The History of William Webb

PREPARED FOR PUBLICATION
BY
HISTORIC PULISHING

ISBN: 978-1-946640-36-9

HISTORIC PULISHING
©2017 (Edited Materials)

The History of William Webb

The History of William Webb: Composed by Himself

William Webb
b. 1836

THE HISTORY
OF
WILLIAM WEBB,
COMPOSED BY HIMSELF.

DETROIT:
EGBERT HOEKSTRA, PRINTER.
1873.

The History of William Webb

THIS book was composed by WILLIAM WEBB, and written by his wife, containing the life he has went through, his views of the present time, and the future to come. Having been raised in slavery, and having received no education, he hopes, by the sale of these books, to obtain his schooling for he is not able to read, up to the present time.

The History of William Webb

HISTORY OF WILLIAM WEBB.

As I am getting along in age, it makes me look back to the days of my youth, and makes me remember my parents, and though they were in slavery, and I was born a slave, I often study how strict my parents reared me, although they were slaves. My mother taught me there was a Supreme Being, that would take care of me in all my trials; she taught me not to rebel against the men that were treating me like some dumb brute, making me work and refusing to let me learn to read. Parents have a great responsibility resting upon them, in rearing their children in the fear of the Lord. Parents ought never to teach their children to hate another race of people.

When I was between nine and ten years of age, I often went by myself to study how wicked the people were getting to be. I wandered through the fields and saw how the slaveholders were treating the women in slavery, and rearing their own children as slaves, and selling them, and saw the cruel whipping. I stood by, and the thought came to mind then, of the Supreme Being my mother had taught me about; I looked to the heavens and cried out Lord if you rule this earth, why do not you deliver us from this cruel bondage. I heard a voice say, I will be with you and your race of people; so when I heard that voice, I remained silent. I went and told my mother what I had heard, and my mother said, "my son, that was God who spoke to you, that time will come, though I may not live to see it. She told me I would travel far and near, that I would travel more than all the rest of the children. In your travels, you will hear a great many different doctrines, but the voice you heard, will be with you in all your travels. She said, "son, always remember the love of God, He can comfort you, when everyone has forsaken you."

At the time this happened, I was living in Georgia. The master I belonged to moved to Mississippi. My father said to his children, I am going to part from all of you, I have heard so much about Mississippi; I shall not go with you, so he called his children about him the night we were going to leave, and told us to remember what he had taught us, and how he had tried to bring us up right, and he told us all to mind our mother. We told our mother that we might never see her again in this world, but if we don't we hope to meet you in heaven. My mother burst out crying. My father went down to the Welonco River, and went on board a boat with his brother, sailed with him one year and two months. They fell out about something one day, and his brother betrayed him to the speculators. He escaped twice after that, and shortly after that he departed from this world, and we moved to Italia Country, which was in the middle of the State of Mississippi, and there I witnessed things I never expected to see. I have seen men and women tied down over a log, with their feet on one side and their arms on the other side, and they would whip them from their head to their feet, and their flesh was cut till they had to rub them with salt and red pepper to keep the flies from blowing them. I have been around the plantations and seen men and women, with the worms crawling in their flesh, and many of them died from the effects of their cruel whipping and want of attention. From day break till 8 o'clock, you could have heard the bull whip cracking, and the groans of the sufferers. Then when I saw all this, the voice I heard in Georgia, came to my mind, and what my mother had told to me, and then I began to think what I should do to be

11

delivered from this cruel treatment, and the thought came to me to go out in the woods, where nobody was traveling; as I thought, so I did, and I dug me a den in the ground. I had not ran away, I was only fixing a place, in case I was obliged to run away, and then I made me another den, so that if they found the first cave, I would have another one to go to for safety.

When I was fifteen years old, I began to think more than ever of what my mother had taught me about a Supreme Being that ruled the whole earth, was true, and I began to look to him to deliver me out of all my trials and temptations. From that day, I always believed that I would be delivered from the rule of man on this earth. As soon as I felt in my heart, that God was the Divine Being that I must call on in all my troubles, I heard a voice speak to me, and from that time I lost all fear of men on this earth.

On the plantation where I lived, there were twenty-five persons, and a great sickness passed through the land, everybody was sick on the plantation but me. I remained in good health, but my trust in the Lord was so great, that I did not think the sickness could come near me. I was the only person there was to wait on them all, and I could hear them say, one to the other, that they were so afraid that I would take sick, and every morning they would ask me how I felt. I told them that I was well, that the good man was watching over me and keeping all sickness from me, and they said, "did not he say the good man was watching over him, I wonder what makes him think that," and they asked me what did I know about the good man. I told them that a voice always followed me and said that, I will always be with you in all of your trials. They said, who told you that it was the good man that spoke. I told them that I had a feeling come over me when I heard that voice, that told me that it was God that spoke to me, and the people told me if I always listened to that voice, I would be right in everything.

I had been living with my mother and brothers and sisters up to this time. My mistress died, and shortly after, my master died. It was the custom to divide the slaves among the children the old master left behind, so we were all parted from one another, and there was great sorrow among us to think we had to be parted from one another, and my mother said, "children the time has come when we must be separated, I do not know whether we will ever see each other in this world, but if we do not, I hope to meet you in heaven. But when the time came for us to be divided, we lived seven miles apart, but the children were not married, so they hired us out. It fell to my lot to be hired to a very hard slave-holder, and I experienced hardships I had never known before. I had to work from day break till seven and eight o'clock at night. Many days I have looked at the sun, wishing it was time for it to go down, so that I might rest from my labor. Many times, I was so tired from working, that I laid right down on the ground and went to sleep, and when I awoke, many times I was wet with dew. Many Sundays I have worked all day in the field, but I trusted in the Lord through all my hardships, and he brought me safely through. I never had a day's sickness all the time I was hired out, for five months. The next time I was hired to one of the daughters of my old master. While I lived with her, I had a very good time, it felt like home to me. I lived with her one year.

Old master's son married a girl from Kentucky, and he took me with him to Kentucky. We moved with an ox team. We were five weeks on the road, from Mississippi to Kentucky, Warren County, between Bowling Green and Shaker Town. When we got the wagon loaded, I bid the folks all farewell. We started about ten o'clock, it was in the winter, and at four o'clock, we camped out for the night. It was very rainy, and so stormy that we did not rest much, being afraid that some of the trees would fall on us and crush us to death. When day broke, we started on our journey. We passed through many large plantations during our travels, and the same cruelty was going on in every one of them. The whip and whipping post were used as an everyday occurrence. There were lanes running through great plantations that took us sometimes all day to get to the end of them. Traveling all the time, and seeing such cruelty going on at each side of me, I said, good man, how long shall this cruel bondage last. I found that when I called on God in my trials, he sent comfort to my heart, and told me the time would come, when I would be free in this world. The water was at high tide, and had washed the bridges away, so that the team could not get over, so we had to unpack the things and carry them across on our backs. After we had carried the things across the creek, we started the oxen into the water, and made them swim across the creek, and then we loaded the wagon and started on our journey. My master took sick with consumption on the road, and we had to stop a week on the road. We came to an old-fashioned meeting house, that had been deserted and when we found it, the hogs had taken possession of it. We carried my master into this old house, and we inquired in the neighborhood, where we could find a doctor, and they said there was one about three miles from the place where

14

we were stopping. He came and attended to my master till he got better, and then we started on our road again. We met great droves of colored people, that put me in mind of a large drove of sheep or other cattle being driven to the market to sell them. When they sold any of the slaves, they examined his teeth and mouth, just like they do horses. We reached our journey's end quite safe. His father-in-law was a tobacco dealer, and he went to Bowling Green, and took possession of his plantation, and raised a tobacco crop that season.

I saw something different here, than I had ever seen before. The speculators went round buying colored people-- even little children. They had large plantations of them and when they got a large drove of them together, they shipped them down South.

I had a very good time myself, while I was in Kentucky. It was better than any State I had lived in yet. It was a sea-port where they raised colored people and shipped them to other States.

When my time was almost up, my master took a notion to move back to Mississippi. I was sorry to go back, for where I lived was better than where I came from. My master bought a span of mules and moved back to Mississippi with mules. We were only two weeks on the road back to Mississippi, the mules made a quick trip.

When I got back to Mississippi again, I was hired out to another hard slave holder. He told me he had heard of me for a long time, and he always wanted to get hold of me, so he asked me did I want to live with him. I told him I thought we could get along together, if we both acted right. I had a great many trials but by the mercy of God, I got through with them all.

In the State of Mississippi, if a man was caught out without a pass from his master, he was punished. When it got so bad about our going out at night, I thought that a crowd of us men would get together and try and put an end to it. We knew the road the patrol took, so we tied a lot of grapevines across the road. We went up the road about a hundred yards, so that they could see us and take after us with horses, and then we ran back and hid among the grapevines. The vines we had tied across the road, threw down the patrol's horses, and threw them off, and played the wild with them, and a great many of them got hurt, so they thought that it was bad policy to be riding about after the colored people after night, so it broke them up in that neighborhood.

It was a rule for the overseer to come at nine o'clock, and lock the cabin doors, belonging to the colored people. He would call each person by their name, and they had to answer, to let him know they were in their cabins. We had old-fashioned dirt chimneys; we would crawl out upon the roof, get down, and be away till nearly day-break. Then I began to thing how much better the State of Kentucky was than Mississippi. It seemed as though people were free in Kentucky, when compared with Mississippi. I lived out that year, without a day's sickness, the year was almost out, and Christmas was at hand. This day was looked for by the colored people with much rejoicing, for then they had one week holiday to spend as they pleased. They made great preparations for balls and tea parties. We would walk nine and ten miles to a ball, and dance all night. The slaveholders would come to the ball and look on, and it seemed as if they enjoyed it as much as the colored people; and so we spent the week. New Year's Day, was the day for us to be hired out, and we all met at a little town called Mayfield. We all stood up on a block to be cried off to the highest bidder; and there was a great many mean slave-holders there, and it made me tremble every time they made a bid for me, because I knew what kind of men they were, so at last, I was knocked down to one of them, so he took hold of me, and turned me around, and looked at me, and said, "boy, I want you to be at my house to-morrow morning." Next morning I was on the spot, and he began to lay down his laws to me. He told me I must not look inside of a book or paper, and said I must never be in the company of any of the poor white people, they might put some mischief in your head that would be the cause of your death. You must be up at the first sound of the horn in the morning, and be out in twenty minutes. No talking in the field, unless it goes through the overseer. You must never be out at night, unless you have a pass from the overseer, and if you break any of these laws, it is two hundred lashes on your naked back, and afterwards they will rub salt and red pepper in the stripes. After that, he told me to go to work. The rest of the hands were rolling logs and burning brush. No day passed away, but you could hear the whip-lash sounding all through the plantation. I lived through all the cruel treatment. One night, I thought I would steal out and enjoy myself, and, as I was walking along, I heard something that sounded like a person running, I jumped back into the bush a few feet from the road, and I saw that it was but one man, and I called him, and found that it was a friend of mine. He told me he had seen a spirit, and it had

17

frightened him, he had often told me that he saw spirits, but I never believed him, for I had traveled as much as any man, and I had never saw any yet; I asked him to go back and show it to me. He went back, but he made me walk in front, while he was behind. We came to the spot where he had seen the spirit, and when I was within a few feet of the place, heard something groaning as though in great pain. Then I began to think there were spirits, sure enough. I ventured up to it, and poked it with my walking cane, when the spirit turned, out to be a pig with the cholera. I then turned to him, and said, "that was the kind of spirits one-half the people saw, which, on, examination turned out to be some living thing on this earth. I then started to the place where I was going to spend part of the night, and when I got there, I had a good time, as I thought. I returned back home, and found all things well. When I went to work in the morning, the overseer asked me how I liked the place, I told him I like it tolerably well, so far. He told me that my master had said I was a very bright and honest-looking boy, and to treat me well. He said, I am going to put you foremost on the plantation, and I look to you to keep everything correct.

Everything went on well, except the cruel treatment, which went on. After some time, I thought I would take another good, time to myself, so I stole out by climbing out of the chimney. I had a good time that night, and returned early, and found things all well. The time for gathering cotton had come, and every man had an acre of cotton to gather, and, if he failed in his task, woe be to him. I went out to spend another night. They had patrolmen out to catch the colored people, and if they found them, they would whip them. I was enjoying myself to the best of my ability, when we heard three knocks at the door, and the patrol said, "open the door." I knew if they caught me, they would use me very rough. I began to think what I should do to escape from them. An old-fashioned shovel stood in the corner, I ran to he fire-place and filled the shovel with fire and ashes, and when they opened the door, I threw the shovel, ashes and fire, at them, and while they were busy brushing the fire from themselves, I escaped. I thought I had better return home, for my enjoyment was broken up for that night.

I went to hear preaching one Sunday. This preacher was engaged by the slaveholders to preach to the colored people; the text he took was, "to be obedient to your master and mistress," so that was his sermon; although he told us if we minded our master and mistress, we would be rewarded. I thought that was good preaching at that time. I heard the colored people sending up prayers to God to relieve them from the cruel bondage they were suffering. They went out in the woods, and offered up prayers; they even prayed when they were picking cotton, or any other kind of work. I passed things that year without a single day's sickness.

Good old Christmas was at hand, when we enjoyed ourselves so much. The week passed away, and New Year's Day, and the hiring out day came around again. We met again, at the same place. Many of the slaves were sold that day, and I was watching when it would be my turn to be cried off. When I was place on the block, my heart was trembling, for fear I should be hired to some hard master. They continued bidding on me, and at last I was hired to the highest bidder, for nine months. He was a tolerably fair man, and he told me to be there the next morning bright

19

and early. He was not a very hard slave holder; he did not give me any strict orders.

Time passed on very well those nine months. One night I thought I would go out and have a good time to myself. In going along the road, I met another friend of mine, he was very much alarmed at a ghost he had seen in passing by an old-fashioned churchyard. I told him to go back with me, I wanted to see a ghost. When we got to the churchyard, I saw two long things lying on the graves. When I come near to them, they proved to be two large oxen. I told my friend to always examine what a thing really was, before he got frightened. I went on my road, and I got to the place I was going to, and, it being Saturday, I spent the whole night. I returned home in the morning, and found all things right.

On Sunday, our master read his Bible to his hands, and explained it to us, the best he knew how, but we did not understand him.

In the course of time, we had a camp meeting, close by where I was then living. I thought that was my chance to make a few dimes, so I baked a few ginger cakes about as big as a common spelling book, and asked ten cents apiece. I stationed myself by a spring where the people came to drink. The spring was quite a ways from the campground. A good many of the colored people had whiskey to sell, and I saw they were selling the whiskey a heap faster than I was selling my cakes. After the camp meeting had lasted three days, I heard such a shouting, I thought I would go and see what was the matter. I went up there; they were falling over the benches and falling and jumping. I was amazed. I thought at first, they were all drunk, there had been so much whisky sold, so I went back and got a jug of whisky, and commenced to sell it at ten cents a drink, and had no trouble in selling it as fast as I could hand it out. I sold many gallons. I saw that the head leaders at the camp meeting drank whisky, and it appeared to me that liquor had more to do with these people than the spirit of God. I made upwards of forty-two dollars by selling whisky, and returned back home a rich man, as I thought. That was the most money I ever had of my own, so I used my money the best I knew how. My master asked me how I liked the camp meeting. I said I liked it good. I told him if there were many more camp meetings, I expected to get rich. He asked me if I made any money selling ginger cakes, for his wife helped me make them, and I told him I sold a few, but I found out selling whisky paid the best.

There arose a great trouble in the Southern States, about Fremont running for President. The people commenced having great meetings, and they would make speeches, saying the streets would run with blood before the North should rule. That was the first the colored people knew about another Nation wishing for the slaves to be free, and the scales of ignorance fell from their eyes. The name of Fremont sounded in every colored person's heart. They understood the name of Fremont meant freedom to them. They held great meetings, and had speeches among themselves, in secret. They knew if the slaveholders heard about them holding meetings it would be death to them. They would hold meetings, and pray. They put all their trust in Fremont to deliver them from bondage. And when Fremont ran and was defeated, a great anger arose among the colored people, but the slaveholders were rejoiced to

21

think that he got defeated. Then the slaves began to study how they would get free, and they held a meeting to try some other way to get free from their cruel bondage. They would make speeches among themselves, to the best of their knowledge about what steps they would take. Some would speak about rebelling and killing, and some would speak, and say, "wait for the next four years." They said they felt as if the next President would set the colored people free. They sent word to me to be sure and be at the meeting. The place where they met, was about fourteen miles from the place I lived at, and being tired, I sat down and listened to them, speaking before they called me. The name of Webb sounded through the house, to get up and make a speech; I said if they would let me lay the foundation of the meeting, I would join them, and they all agreed with me, so I arose and said to the crowd they must form a company, and surround the place of meeting, to watch that none of the slave holders came upon us by surprise, and they agreed to it. I said I would go myself, and station a guard around so as to be sure in my own mind, that all things were right. I took them three hundred yards from the spot, and stationed them around, and I took another squad and stationed them a hundred yards further off than the first guard. I told the outsiders if they saw any of the patrol coming, to give a yell and run so the rest of us might have a chance to run; and I told those that I had stationed first, not to yell unless the patrol came that way; I told the guard to watch, and whoever saw the patrol first, to give the alarm. Then I went back to the meeting and they asked me if I had all things right; I told them I had all things right outside, but there was another thing, I wanted them all to take an oath that they would never let the secret out, and everybody that was willing to take the oath, to hold up both hands. All at the meeting held up their hands, and I said, "if anyone was found out telling the secret, we would put him in a bag with a rock tied around his neck and sink him in a creek." That was agreed to. Then I selected eight more men, four of them walked back and forth to the guard, so they would know from which way the alarm came; and the other four I stationed around the place of meeting. I told them I thought I had everything fixed to carry on our meeting with satisfaction. I then called on one of the speakers to address the crowd, and that I would speak next. He got up and spoke, to the best of his knowledge. He said he thought when Fremont ran, we would be free, but we were still bending under the whiplash. He said he thought there would be steps taken for our freedom; he said he saw a light in the land that told him he would be free yet; he said if all had the same mind he had, all the land would be slain in less time than a week; he said he was as sure as the sun rose and set, that light would keep shining till we all would enjoy it, so he sat down and they called on me again; but I was so much interested in the speaking, that I called on another man to speak. He arose and said, I am glad to see you all gathered here to-night, this looks like free life. I am forty years of age, and I never felt so much like being free, as I do to-night to think we are talking about being free, and I hope you will all remain like this until we get free, for we are going to have our freedom. I felt it my heart that the name Fremont meant freedom. He thought he was a glorious man, and he thought, now the question of freedom was started, it would never stop till the colored man was freed from his bondage. He sat down and they called on another man to speak. He got up and said he had no thought of addressing the crowd that night, but he said everything looked so strong about the meeting, that he did not feel afraid to speak, but he felt as if he was two feet higher; he was so proud to think we were making preparations for a free life. That good man, who ran for President wanted to free us, and he felt that our freedom was at hand. I hope he may live forever, and never die. We met that night, to take steps for our freedom and I do not know what steps to take unless we rebel against the slaveholders, although I am fifty-two years old, I hope I will live to see all the colored people free; I feel as if I should see it, and we believed we would, if it is the Lord's will, and he sat down. Then they called for Webb again, so I arose and told them, as so many had spoken before I got up, I did not have much to say about this great cause, but I said they had sent me word to attend the meeting, and I said I would come if possible; but I felt like the speakers that spoke before I got up. I told them we must be cautious in holding this meeting, that the slaveholders may not know it. Every time you hold a meeting, you ought to put out a gang of men to watch, that none of the patrol should come upon us unawares; and you ought to single out some men to speak in different places, so that those who could not reach the place of meeting, might be instructed in the great work that is going on in the land, trying to free the colored people. I told them I had a heap to say, but as it was drawing near to day break, and some of us had a long way to go, I thought it best to break the meeting up for this time; but we would make arrangements to meet the next Saturday night, and I hope all I have said will be carried out, about placing a guard around our meeting place. I expect to be with you next Saturday, if nothing happened, more than I knew of at present, for I expect to leave you all, very soon. I expect to go to Kentucky, and if I do, I will establish headquarters there so as to get news from there to

Mississippi. We can not do much unless we can send word all over. We all must know, before we make a movement. I think we ought to make this place the headquarters, that all the news be sent to the headquarters, and they will tell others what to do. Then I said we have had a good time, no patrol have bothered us. I feel truly thankful. Old Uncle Ned said we ought to send up a prayer in remembrance of this night. Then the meeting broke up, and we scattered in all directions, going toward home. The next six days seemed a long time passing away, I was so anxious to be with all of them at the meeting then. I heard a whisper going around among the slaveholders that the slaves like to have got free. If Fremont had been elected, they would have been free. I began to think that something more than common was going on, and I was rejoiced over the meeting we had, and wishing from one day to another, that Saturday night would come, because the time was up that I was hired for, and I expected to have a good time attending the meetings in different parties. The long wished for night arrived, I passed out without having a day's sickness. The night of the meeting came around, and I was there according to promise.

They had guards out, and I was very proud to see them have the guard strewed around. We all met again with much pleasure. A great many of them got up and spoke to the best of their knowledge, and the meeting passed off all right. All of them were anxious to hear me, seeing I was going to leave them in a very short time, so they began calling for Webb. I arose with much joy; I told them I was glad to meet with them once more, for I felt as if it was the last time. I told them I expected to leave them all. for I was going back to Kentucky again, but I told them to keep up the great cause and to tell one another we expected to be free. One of the speakers thought it would be best to start out and slay, not sparing women or children. I told them I did not think that plan would do; I told him all the way that could be done with justice would be to establish a king in every State, and let every king make his laws in his own State, and let his place be the headquarters. I thought it best for each king to appoint a man to travel twelve miles, and then hand the news to another man, and so on, till the news reached from Louisiana to Mississippi, and then if we were to rebel, we would rebel in all the States at one time, so the white people would not have a chance. Then I said, we had better make old Uncle Ned one of the kings, as he knew the whole country around, and had lived in it two years at a time. Then Uncle Ned rose up and said he knew a man he could send all the way through and establish other men to carry the news twelve miles. I told Uncle Ned that he was a king bee, and any man told the secret out, to bind a bag around him and fill it full of rocks, and sink him in the creek; and I told Uncle Ned that as he knew the country so well, we would try and get word to one another when I found out what part of Kentucky I was going to. He said he had a friend in Nashville, Tennessee, that he would send word to. Then I told them, that I had told them all I had to say, so we talked the matter over to the best of our ability, and after Uncle Ned had offered up a prayer, the meeting was dismissed, and everybody returned home. They all bid me farewell, Then I returned to my old master, who was waiting until my time was up to return to Kentucky. He told me he was very happy to see me, and made me a present of five dollars in silver, and told me to go around and see my friends, and bid them good-bye. He made preparations to start to Grey's County Kentucky. I went round and saw my mother, and my brothers and sisters. When I parted from my mother, she told me to be of good cheer, for if she never saw me in this world, she hoped to meet me in another world, where we would never be parted. I returned home.

We started for Greys Co., Kentucky, the weather was fair and we moved on. I was rejoiced to think I was going back to Kentucky. I enjoyed myself all the way; the weather was fair and we were still moving on. We landed in Greys County in three weeks, and had good luck all the way. My master got him a place for one year. When he had settled himself, I began to look around for my colored friends. I had been there two months, and had not seen more than a dozen. I went nine and ten miles out, and I found plenty of them, whole plantations. I began to introduce myself around among them, but as I came from Mississippi, they looked down on me. Then I thought I would tell them what we were trying to do in Mississippi. I commenced telling them, but I saw it would not pay at that time. Then I thought I would drop that subject. I saw that they looked down on me more than ever. I returned back home again. I studied all that week till Sunday came, what course I would take, so the thought came to me that when Sunday came to go back in the woods and dig me a den. I hunted the woods through till I found a suitable place for my den, and I marked it out. I returned home and studied another week whether I had better dig me a den in the woods. When the next Sunday came I carried the tools with me and dug my den, so if any thing happened, I would have a place to drop back on. It was on the side-hill, and if it rained the water would run down. After I had dug the den, I raked leaves, brush and logs over the dirt so that it would not be noticed. When everything was completed, I returned home again. The next Sunday I thought I would go out and try my friends again. I passed off the time first rate, but not as well as I would have liked to. When night came on, I returned home again, and studied all that week what I would put before my friends next Sunday. My master asked me how I liked the people out this way. I told him I liked the people pretty well, but not as well as I would like to. I told him my friends looked down upon me because I came from Mississippi. He asked me what was the reason they looked down upon me. I told him I did not know, but I thought it was because Mississippi had a hard name. When Sunday came, I thought I would try my friends again, so I asked them if they ever heard any talk about getting free. They told me it was death to talk about freedom in this country. Then I began to tell them about people having a sleight of hand in making people good. They asked me what kind of sleight of hand. I told them sleight of hand to make our masters good, and they said there had been men through the county, giving sleight of hand, but it never done any good, so I told them I thought with other strength, I could give them sleight of hand that would cause them to live more happy than they had been living. I inquired of them where the meanest plantation was that they knew of, so then they told me about the meanest plantation they ever heard of, they said there was cruel whipping carried on, and all other kinds of cruel treatment till that plantation was not respected at all, even the colored people that lived there, were not respected because they belonged to that plantation. I told them where I came from, all plantations were treated cruel, but as there was only one plantation in Kentucky where the slaves were treated cruel, I thought I could remedy that. They asked me how. I told them that something always followed me, and if I could use that, I thought I could make that plantation good. They said, to-night we will carry you down and make you acquainted with that plantation. I told them I would be most happy to go, so when night came they took me to that plantation and introduced me to the people, and I sat down and enjoyed myself. I saw there was great anger among them about the way they were treated. I felt then that I was at home, and I visited from one house to another. I found some old people praying that did me good, I saw they had a knowledge of what was following me, so the friend told them I was a peace maker, that I came on purpose to make peace on that plantation, and the news went out from one cabin to another, that the peace maker had come, so in less time than an half an hour I was surrounded with the friends telling their cause, so many old men and women said we have been praying for you many days, to come and move our masters, so they were so overjoyed they killed a lamb that we might enjoy ourselves, and the lamb was put in a dirt oven and baked. While it was baking, we talked about their cruel treatment and what they had went through. I felt as if I were at home, I thought I had come across a streak of luck. Then old Aunt Mary called out that supper was ready, which was about twelve o'clock at night, so three ladies dressed in white came to take me to supper. They asked me to say the blessing, but not being accustomed to ask a blessing, I did not know what to say. I thought I was trumped, but the words entered into my mind to say, Lord this night we eat this lamb, restore peace on this plantation, so we eat and made merry and enjoyed ourselves over the table, and then I returned home. Some of the friends went home with me, I thought if I could gain the good will of that plantation, I would gain the rest of the people, so I went to work in earnest, and I sent up many prayers to God through the week, to deliver that plantation from its cruel treatment. The head leader of the colored people on that plantation came to seem me about the middle of the week, he told me he had lived on that plantation for fifteen years, and he said he had never seen such a change as had been there that week, and that lifted me up then, and I saw that it was good to have faith in God, so I told him to go back and tell all the people on the plantation to go down on their knees every morning, and ask God to deliver that plantation from the evil that was in it, and he said he would. Then I saw there was something else I must do to gain their attention, so I got a parcel of roots and put them in a small bag about as big as my thumb and sewed them up. Saturday night came, and I was proud of it. I went back to the plantation to see how times were, and they were all glad to see me. They met me by scores, and I was glad to see them, for I thought I had hit the right place, so they talked and told me about what times they had that week; they said that was the best week they had for many a day. Then I trusted in God more than ever, and they had a fine supper prepared, so I eat and enjoyed myself. Then I turned into a room in company with a good many ladies, and we talked and had a sociable time, till it began to be late in the night. I then told them I had an object I wanted to act before I went to bed, so I called twelve of them together and I had twelve of those little bags of roots, and I gave them to the twelve persons and placed them in their hands, and told them we would march around the house seven times, and I told them to shake these bags each time they marched around the house, and say peace be with us. They did so, and returned back in the house. I told them every morning when they got up, to shake those bags in the direction of their master's

30

house and say, Lord peace be with us this day, and I told them not to tell the rest about the bags of roots they had, but to carry them in their pockets all the time, and I told them to tell all the rest to say peace be unto us to-day, as soon as they arose in the morning. Then I told the twelve men I was from Mississippi, and they were doing, great works in Mississippi, and I am here on purpose to let the people know what we are doing in Mississippi, but I am not ready to let you know yet. I want to find out how truthful you all are, and how much dependence I can put in you all. The head man I elected, was named John. Then John said the men he had in view he had known for fifteen years, and they could be trusted with a secret, so I told him I would make him head ruler of that department, and the meeting broke up. The ladies had apples and all such notions prepared for us and so we returned back to have a sociable time; then I went to bed. The next morning was Sunday morning, they had a nice breakfast prepared for me, and all things were peaceful on the plantation, and they had great faith, so the day was passing off and I had a very pleasant time. The old master of the plantation saw me around the cabins and he made it his business to come down to see who I was. I began to think some of the people must have betrayed me, for the colored people said he was not in the habit of coming down to the cabins on Sunday. He said he saw a strange man there that he had never saw before, and he wanted to see him. I came forth, and he said to me, how are you boy. He said he never came around his cabins, but he saw a me there a stranger, and I drew his attention, and he had come down to have a chat with me, and he asked me what county I was from, and I told him I was from Mississippi, and he asked me how I came up here. I told him my master moved up here. Then he asked me how I

31

liked Kentucky. I told him I liked it tolerably well so far. He asked me how I liked the colored people beside those of Mississippi. I told him I liked them first rate. He asked me if the people in Kentucky were as cruel to their slaves as they were in Mississippi. I told him no, but I had heard around he was the meanest man there was. He said, ah! indeed, he said he had been very bad but he had changed his opinion, he did not think the same as he did two weeks ago. I asked him what was the cause of his changing his opinion. He said he had a heavy burden on his mind for the last week, and his mind became a trouble to him. I asked him what was the cause of that. He said he did not know. but he thought once his niggers were trying to poison him. I told him it might be the Lord was working on him. I asked him if he felt sorry for the sins he had committed. He said yes, but his niggers troubled him more than anything else; he said, at night when I am asleep it seems as if my niggers are standing around me. I told him it might be that there was something telling him to treat his slaves better. He said he had changed his mind from what it had been. He asked me if I had any education. I said to him, no, I did not have a bit, I did not know A from B. He said to me, you are the brightest looking boy I ever saw in my life. He said, I have a good many girls here, you can come and see them whenever your master will let you come. Then he parted from me. I then summoned my twelve men together, to have a talk over the subject, and they had more faith than they had before. I was much lifted up, I saw it was good to trust in God. Then they began to reason among themselves about the bags of roots they had. I heard them talking about the roots. I asked them what they thought the bags of roots were for. One said it was to conjure old master; another said he thought it was to draw master down. I could talk with him then. I told them those roots were to make them faithful when they were calling on the Supreme Being, and to keep your mind at work all the time. We parted after that. By that time, the ladies had everything fixed for another sociable talk. Then I enjoyed myself the rest of the evening. I had traveled a good deal, and could pass off time very well. We enjoyed dinner, and after that we took a walk out. They showed me the fields and the little patches they had, and enjoyed myself that evening. When night came, I called twelve men together to give them advice before I left. I told them that through faith, you have got your master moved; by faith he will continue on. I told them to say every morning, peace be with us to-day, Oh! Lord. Then I saw they had great faith. I was much rejoiced, for I thought I would have a good foothold to carry out my other points. I told them I must go home, but I would come back next Saturday night, if the Lord was willing; to be of good cheer. Then I returned back home again. My master asked me how I was getting along in enjoying myself now. I told him I enjoyed myself first rate, that the master at the plantation where I went, said I could come and see the girls. I was very much pleased, I was overjoyed at my trip, for I was gaining ground. I kept my faith stronger than ever. My heart was so much overjoyed. I was wishing Saturday would make haste and come, but it came at last, and I started for the plantation. They met me with gladness. I told the head man to call the twelve men together for business. He called them together. I asked them how things had passed off that week. They said all things had passed off good, that they had enjoyed themselves better than they thought they ever could with that master. They told me their master had questioned them very closely about me. He asked them what I talked about the most. They told him the most I was talking about was of God. Then he told them he thought from the appearance of my face, I was a good man. I told them to be truthful and keep up the good work they had begun, and they need never fear death. We parted then for pastime. I had a good time with the ladies. I had a very pleasant time that evening, and all day Sunday.

I returned home. I told my master I had a much better time out here, than I expected, among the colored friends. About the middle of the week, that gentleman came down to see my master. He told him his boy was coming to his house to see his girls, and if my master had no objection, he would like to have him come. My master told him that his boy and himself were raised up playfellows together, and he thought a great deal of me. He told my master that was the brightest looking boy he had ever seen. He said he thought I was an educated man.

The week passed away, and Saturday night came, and I was anxious to return again. I called my men together once more, and asked them how they were getting along, and they said all things were well. I asked them then, if they ever thought anything about getting free. They said they had been thinking they would be free, for a long time, and praying that they would live to see it. I asked them how they expected they would ever get free. One thought of rebelling and killing all the whites which he thought was about all the way he could get free; another said he did not think it could be done in that way. I asked them if they ever heard anything about Fremont. They said they had heard about him, but they said he did not get elected. They thought it would not do any good now. I told them that Fremont was a small light, and it would keep burning till it was spread over the whole world. I told them I would tell them more whenever they were able to bear it, and then the meeting broke up. The ladies had prepared a nice supper, and I enjoyed it. When it was over, I went into another room to have a sociable chat with the ladies. They wanted me to talk about the free life that was coming. I told them I did not know that I could talk to them as I would wish to, but I was acquainted with them enough to tell them what I thought. I was sure all the colored people would be free in a very short time. Down in Mississippi, where I came from, we understand things pretty well, we see how things are going on. Slaveholders down in Mississippi are very uneasy, and by what I saw, I think there is a great light coming, and it will be here sooner than we expect. Old Aunt Mary said she had been praying many days for deliverance. She said, in her dreams she saw great hosts of men drawn up together. She said she heard a voice say, "this is to free you." I told old Aunt Mary I had been hearing that voice from my youth up, and I was sure I would live to see it. Keep your faith, and it will surely come. I find faith the best after all. It is by faith that I am here now, trying to build up. Never forget to pray and trust in the Supreme Being, who stands in the midst of heaven. I hope you will not betray me, for you know that if anybody was going to burn your house down, you would want to know it, so that you could get away in time. This light is given to us, to know that free life is coming. This is my purpose, to warn you all to be ready to receive your prize that is coming. I would tell you more, but I cannot at the present time. We dropped that subject, and the ladies passed the refreshments around, and I enjoyed myself and had a good time. The evening Passed away pleasantly, and I went to bed.

35

Next morning everything looked lovely, and I thought I was progressing in strength. The day passed away first rate. When night came, I called my twelve men together for business. They sent me word they were all ready. I asked them if they knew of any other plantation that was as bad as this one. They said they knew of another one that was very bad. I told them I would like to get another place as mean as this plantation, for I wanted to spread the faith farther on, for faith never stops in one place. I would like them to pick out the worst place they could find and carry me to it the next week. Then I told them I was glad to think I had men that I could put faith in, because I was very much worried when I first came here. But now I am highly lifted up; and having heard that this place was the worst place there was, I came here to show people that by faith, many things can be moved. I would like you all to testify how different things are now, to what they were before I came. John said he had never seen a place improve so much in so short a time. It seemed as if they were free, compared to what it used to be. Then they all got up and spoke about the great change there had been. I was well lifted up then. I told John to tell his best friends how things had changed here, and how all things prospered. Then I told them to keep their faith and keep doing as I commanded you till I tell you to change, and the meeting broke up, and we passed off the rest of the evening in a sociable way, and I had a good time among the ladies. I returned home, and my master asked me how I was getting along. I told him I was getting along nicely. He said he was glad to hear it. He said I had left all my folks in Mississippi, and he was afraid I would not be satisfied. I asked him how he liked it out here. He said that he liked it first rate. I studied all that week what I would put before the people when Saturday night came. The week passed off, and my mind was all taken up in this great work I was in. Then I began to think how I would interest the people in the neighborhood, so as to carry out some of my other points. I planned everything ready for Saturday night.

Saturday night came again, and I was on the spot again. I called the men together, and asked them how they got along through the week. They said all things were right, that all things were working faithfully. I asked John if he had spread the news around among his best friends. He told me he had, and he expected a good many to be on hand. I asked him whether he could depend on the men he had asked. He said they were all to be depended upon. I told him I was much rejoiced to think he had found men he could trust. I will give you a little sketch of what we have been doing in Mississippi. We thoroughly understand about our freedom down there. We have established meetings all through Mississippi, that everybody might know what was coming. I tell you, friends, this light is coming to all men; it has grown so strong in Mississippi, that the slaveholders are roused up. They have great meetings to guard against this, but as sure as Heaven stands, they are not able to stand against them. There has been too many prayers sent up to God, and I am confident that he has heard them, although I cannot hear how they are getting along yet, but if you all will only be faithful to me, I will learn how they are getting along in different States. I left word and they will send the news on through as soon as I am able to receive it. I would like to hear how many you have told to meet here on Sunday. John said, I do not know how many will come, but I spoke to twelve or thirteen to meet here, and Peter offered up a prayer that every one might be true, and put his shoulder to the wheel to push it on. Then the meeting broke up, and I had a pleasant time. We had supper, and I passed off the rest of the evening with much enjoyment.

Sunday morning came, and other friends commenced coming together. I began to tell them about the plans I had laid out, and hoping they would take hold likewise. I spent the Sunday making preparations to send news to Nashville, Tennessee, to my friend there. I worked on faithfully for about a month, and got my road completed. I could get news from Mississippi to the headquarters at Kentucky in a very short time. I had friends all over the country. They came miles upon miles to see me. I got news from different States in a very short time. I carried that plan on till the time Lincoln was elected. About seven months before the election of Lincoln, my main master sold me. He said the next President that was elected, would be an Abolitionist, and he thought the colored people would be set free, and that we would sell me, and put the money in his pocket. He sold me for fifteen hundred dollars cash, but I was doing such big business that I did not mind it at all. I was not much pleased with the man that bought me. At that time I was receiving news from a great many States. I astonished the man that bought me, by telling him how things were going on in different States, till he thought I must be a wizard, or something worse. Time passed off very well with me. I had all the business I was able to attend to. After the nomination, we could hear nothing in Kentucky, but the names of Bell and Douglas. There was nothing heard about Lincoln till a while before the election came off. The name of Lincoln going to free the slaves, was the next news heard by the colored people, and the blessed news flew from one State to another, and the colored people all over the State knew who was their friend, and we understood the whole

matter. Then my friend sent me word that they were getting
up soldiers in Mississippi and at other points fixing for war.
Then I sent news for everybody to pray that Lincoln would
be elected. The time passed away, and the election came
off. Lincoln was elected and great thanks went up to the
Lord from the colored people. The next news we heard,
was a great talk about war. That kept growing stronger and
stronger in the land, till we saw that we had to do
something else. We sent out word all over, in all the States,
for the colored people not to take up arms for the
slaveholders. Everything was well understood among the
colored people. My friends sent me word from Mississippi,
that they were up in arms. There was great joy among the
slaves. I was made a spy for the Rebels, but I wanted that
position to gain my other points. I left with a good
understanding with my leaders. I stayed with the rebels
long enough. I had learned all I wanted to know, and I
knew they did not wish me much good will. The next fight
that took place was at Belmont, below Cairo. The
Republicans got beat down there. I wept bitter tears. I
thought then I had better leave. The Yankee soldiers landed
at Paducah, Kentucky. I went down to see them once in a
while. My master thought I was going to run away and stay
with the Yankee soldiers. A crowd of the slaveholders
came and bound me with ropes and carried me down to the
blacksmith shop, and put a shackle around my ankle and a
six-foot chain fastened to it, and he took me to a speculator
nine miles from Mayfield. Those men that carried me to the
speculator, told him to keep me bound tight, for I was a
dangerous man, and if he did not mind, I would get away
from him. We got there on Sunday evening. The speculator
put me up-stairs in his house, and what he was going to do
with me, I am not able to say. That night a voice spoke to

me, saying, "be of good cheer, I will be along with you." When the morning came, it come to my mind what I must do. I went down to breakfast and I said to the old colored woman, who looked as if she was seventy years old, to give me a small file. She got a file and handed it to me and I slipped it into my pocket. She said, you are that man I have heard so much about, and I know you will not betray me. I told her that I would never betray her in the world. Then I called the speculator and told him I wanted to go up-stairs again. He carried me up-stairs, and I told him I would like some rags to wrap around that shackle, it was hurting my ankle. He gave me some rags, and I wrapped them around the shackle and some of the links. I did that in order to file the chain off, and if he came up, I could wrap the rags around and he would not notice it. I filed the chain, and got through about two hours before sunset, and when the chain parted, it appeared to me as if it opened an inch wide. I tied a rotten string around the chain, so that I could break it easy, and I wrapped the rags around it the same as I had them. I looked out of the window and marked out my way to escape, when night came on. When night came, he carried me down to supper. After he carried me down, I told him I wanted to go out in the yard. It was dark, and when the speculator took me out in the yard I broke the chain and escaped. I had twenty-seven miles to go to Paducah, Kentucky, to get to the Union soldiers. The next morning by sunrise, I was in Paducah. When I got there, I went to General Wallace and Captain Lyman, and they asked me if I could cook. I said yes. I still had the iron shackle on my leg. They carried me down to the blacksmith's and had the shackle filed off. Captain Lyman told me he thought I was very ambitious to file that chain and escape. He said he would keep me as long as I would stay with him. They gave me the keys of everything around the house. I was well pleased; but they were taking the slaves back, and I was afraid they would arrest me and carry me back, but Captain Lyman promised me, that they should never get me. In about three days my master came there after me. General Wallace had a guard around his house, and he had to go through the guard before he could get to General Wallace. The guard told General Wallace that a gentleman wanted to speak to him. The General told him to come in. When he came in, the General asked him his business. He said, you have a boy in here I want. The General questioned him very close. The General asked him what I had done to have such iron shackles on my leg. He told him I had not done anything. General Wallace told him he guessed he would keep me, and told him never to come back after me anymore, for if he did he would arrest him. Then I had a good time. I enjoyed myself better than I had ever done before in my life. I sent out word to different points, that I was at the headquarters of the Abolitionists. I told them that Fremont was in Missouri, freeing all the colored people. They sent back a message enjoying the good news, and wishing me much enjoyment that I was free. General Wallace said he was looking for his wife, and when she went back home, I could go with her. He told me I must be a good fellow, and learn to read, for his wife would let me go to school, and I must take care of things around the house. His wife came. He told her about my going home with her, and she was much pleased to have me go with her. Soon after, the order came for us to march around Mayfield in the direction of Fort Henry. General Wallace ordered his wagon to the house, and told me to put all we needed into it, for we would be gone about two weeks. He told his wife to stay there till he came back.

After every thing was ready we moved. We marched through Mayfield, and in the direction of Fort Henry. Provisions began to get short, and I thought I had better go out foraging, as I was so well acquainted with the country, and knew where they kept the provisions. I got sweet potatoes and corn meal, and General Wallace asked me where I made such a raid. I told him I got it from my friends along the road. The next time I made a raid on the chickens. I kept it up till we dropped down four miles below Fort Henry. Then we took the direction of Paducah again, and did not come in contact with the Rebels. General Wallace's wife was glad to see me, and asked me if I took good care of things while I was gone. I told her I did. I got things all straightened up again at the place we were stopping at. They told me to prepare a dinner, for General Grant was coming up from Cairo, and he was going to take dinner with us. I prepared dinner the best I knew how. We received orders to go to Smithflin, a little town twelve miles from Paducah. General Wallace told me to pack up everything in marching order. I got them packed up, and the wagon came to carry them down to the boat. When we arrived at Smithflin, the band met us and marched us up to the hotel. We hunted for a house after we got there, and had some trouble in finding one. One rebel had a house, and General Wallace told him to move out, as he wanted to occupy it for a week or two. Before we got the house fitted up, the orders came about midnight for us to march to Fort Henry. General Wallace told me to pack up the things and be ready to march. General Wallace gave orders to all the troops in Smithflin to march down to the boat, and start for Fort Henry. We landed five miles below Fort Henry. General Wallace marched up on the right of the river, and General Smith marched up on the left side of the river up to

Fort Henry, and they left me on the boat out in the river, and told me to take care of everything. I had a fair sight of all the gunboats on the river and the fight. They commenced fighting with the gunboats. I could see the shells strike the gunboats and dash over them. General Grant came dashing back to the boat I was on, and told the officers that the victory was their's, that the camp was on fire, and a great many of the rebel batteries were disabled, and they could not stand much longer. The Rebels threw a shell through the porthole and it struck the boiler of the gunboat Merrimac and exploded it. General Grant dashed up and examined the boat and told the officers on the boat where I was, that there was not much damage done. The shell struck the boiler and went up through the pilothouse and killed the pilot and scalded a few men. About that time, the Fort surrendered. They said the fight lasted one hour and ten minutes. They took the Rebel General Pendleton prisoner. We landed at Fort Henry, and I went over the ground, and the first thing I saw was one of the Rebel cannon bursted and four men lying dead beside it. I went on farther, and saw all the cabins they had were burning and, some of them knocked to pieces, and a great many dead people scattered around in the Fort. I stood looking on and enjoying our victory. General Wallace took up his headquarters on the same side as he went up on, opposite the Fort. We went in camp. In about eight days the order came for us to march again to Fort Donaldson. General Wallace commanded me to pack up the things and be ready to march. We marched to Fort Donaldson, and at that place we had a very hard fight. I went up close to the place where they were fighting, and I saw one regiment cut all to pieces. I wept with sorrow to see that Union regiment cut up so. The balls kept whistling around me till I dropped back for fear one them would hit me, I went up on the hill. I could see the Rebel cannon firing, and the sharp-shooters would pick them off every time they undertook to load their cannon, till they did not make much headway. I thought I had better drop back to my tent.

On Saturday, they began to fight again. General Grant came to the tent where I was, on Saturday evening, and commanded General Wallace to take the left wing immediately and make a charge on the Fort. General Wallace took the left wing and took the Fort on Saturday evening. I stood on the side of the hill and saw the battle. A great many men fell and the troops fell back and rested Saturday evening. The colored people came to General Wallace's tent that night and said that the Fort had surrendered and a great many of the people were leaving. The next morning a gunboat sent two shells into the Fort, and it did not receive any answer. It dropped back for further orders. One of General Wallace's staff, with a detachment of soldiers went into the Fort to see whether they had surrendered or not. He brought back the news that the Fort had surrendered, and we rejoiced over the fall of the Fort. Generals Pillow and Floyd escaped that night under the banks of the river. The guard did not see them. That night when I was getting supper, I heard them talking among themselves, saying that they were going to take the prisoners to Indianapolis, Indiana. I listened very carefully, for I had heard General Wallace talking about it being a free country. That night after I had got through with supper, I sat down and studied how I could escape along with them. I fixed a plan, that when the prisoners went on board the boat, I would go with them, and pass off for a prisoner.

Monday morning General Wallace ordered me to pack up all the things and start for Fort Henry, where his wife was. I packed everything up and was ready for them to start about twelve o'clock. When the wagon started for Fort Henry, I started for the boat the prisoners were going away on, and passed myself off for a prisoner. We stayed on the boat till we got down to Cairo. When we got down there, the other prisoners had occupied the cars. We had to lay on the boat a day and a night, till a train of cars came from Terre Haute. I saw a man on the boat that lived with me on one of the plantations. He was with one of my old masters. I asked him if his master was living or did he get killed. He said he was down in the hall, and I went down to see him, and he was pleased to see me, and wanted to know how I came to be a prisoner. I told him my other master was going to take me off to some other place, and I got away from him and went to the Union army, and now I was going North. He told me I was going to a free country, and to be industrious and not to claim more than my labor came to. He told me I was a great deal better off than he was. The news came about two o'clock that the cars had come. They marched us off the boat into the cars. Before we started, a bale of hay came for us to lie on. The officers called the prisoners to come out and tear the hay to pieces. There was seven colored men on the cars, and the prisoners told us to go out and tear the bale of hay to pieces, but the officers told us to go back in the car, and ordered the prisoners to come out and get the bale of hay. We started about four o'clock in the morning for Indianapolis, Indiana. All the way along the prisoners quarreled with us, and said they had to break up hay for niggers to lie upon. We got to Terre Haute and stopped there a few minutes. They got a newspaper, and it passed around to nearly every man on the cars, before they could find one able to read it, which was a great astonishment to me. Then we landed in Indianapolis, Indiana, where the prisoners were going to, and everything was prepared for us to take breakfast. We arrived there about seven o'clock in the morning. We all took breakfast and then prepared to march to camp Moulton. All the prisoners marched out, and the colored men along with them, but I remained in the depot. Then I walked out and said to myself, "thank God, I am free." I heard a voice in my ear, say, not free yet; when you depart from sin, then you are free indeed. I was astonished at that voice, and I wondered what it meant. The next thing I began to wonder where I could get a place to stop, as I was a stranger in the city, having no person to tell me anything. I strayed around until I came to a place I thought would suit me, and they let me stop there. After I had been there a week, the cold I had taken broke out on me, and I was very sick. I stopped there about a month, but I got worse instead of better. I went from there to another friend, where I thought they could take better care of me. I was sick there about three months, and received the best of care, and I soon got well and went to work. The first work I began, was chopping wood, but I had so far to walk that I did not make much headway at that and I left it. Sabin Fletcher was graveling a road to make a turnpike, and I went to work for him. He told me he had been a friend to the colored people, and had hid many a one to send them to Canada by the underground railroad. He gave me work, and I worked for him some time. The Southern people were coming to Indianapolis and carrying some of the colored people back again. I thought I had better be traveling. Sabin Fletcher told me there was no danger, that the treaty was broken since the war. But they were taking the colored people and carrying them off without any lawsuit. They took a friend of mine, and I thought it was time for me to go away for fear they might take me the same way. I left the city and went to a place called Cisero, where there was a great many colored people. I remained there about a week. I went from there to New London. It was about harvest time, and I stopped and worked in the harvest fields about a week. I went from there to Peru. I worked around the city for a few days, until I got a chance to work in a wheat field. I got a place, and I had been working about ten days. I was a mile and a half from Peru. A country officer came and arrested me, and carried me about five miles from the city to a Squire. When we got there, (the Squire lived in an old log house), and he took his book down and read the law to me. He read that it was against the law for a white man to give work to a colored man that came from the South, and twelve dollars to five hundred dollars fine or State prison. The man who had hired me paid twelve dollars, and they carried me to Peru to put me in jail, to stand my trial. The news reached the city before I got there, and all the people were prepared to deliver me from this man. When he got to the city, the people said he could not put me in prison, that he must turn me loose, for the Government brought me there, and that he or they could do nothing with me. Then I was free from them. The next morning I went harvesting for another man, and I worked for him about two weeks. Then I went to a hotel to work, and I stayed there till fall, and I left there and came to Detroit, and I went out Fort street west, five miles, and chopped wood all winter. The cemetery is on the spot where I chopped wood. While I was out there a riot occurred in the city, and a great many colored people were fleeing out in the country where I was, and some came to the house where I was stopping to get shelter, both men and women. They said there was a great many bad feeling white people in the neighborhood, and they did not know whether they were safe themselves. I said to Mr. Robinson, we had better be on guard. He asked me what I thought it was best to do. I told him to fix what guns we had in the house, and get what we could in the neighborhood, and he did as I advised him. We put a guard around the place, so that if they saw any people coming, to give the alarm. We sat up and watched all night, but everything went off quiet. I came into the city next day to see what damage they had done. The colored people were very scarce in the places I had been used to see them, and I found that some had run over into Canada, and some of them had run into the woods. A great many gentlemen said it was a great pity they had such a cruel riot, and I asked them if there was no law to prevent such a mob, and they said there was no laws for a mob. I said, I think it is a very queer country that has no law to protect people. They said yes, that is so. The next spring I came into town, and commenced whitewashing, and in working around, I whitewashed for the mayor of the city that spring. We got into a little dispute about the work, and I talked to him with the best manners I could. He ran up to me and told me to hush, that he did not allow niggers to talk to him. I began to think he must have had a hand in the mob. I whitewashed around in the city until harvest time, and then I went out to Ann Arbor. I worked there two weeks, five miles out of the city, and then I took the cars for Michigan City. I went out three miles into the country and went to harvesting again. I worked in that place till harvest was over, and then I took the cars for Indianapolis, Indiana, and I went around to see my friends. They were glad to see me, and I enjoyed myself very much then. I went out on the Madison Road where a lot of colored people were chopping wood, and I chopped wood out there two weeks. I asked the man that owned the wood, what he would take for the down timber and what wood they could not split. He said he would take five dollars an acre. I bought it from him, I sold the chips on the ground, and cut the timber till I had about twenty cords cut, and the wood had risen to three dollars a cord on the ground. I sold my wood to one man, and after that I hired hands to chop for me, and the rest of the colored people that had been chopping in the woods for three months, wondered how I came out there and doubled the money on them. The man I bought the timber from, called me a businessman, and said I had more idea of business, than any man he ever had in the woods. He told me not to hire any of his men, but to go to the city and get men for myself, so as not to injure him in getting in his wood, and I told him I would do as he asked me. I got through chopping all the wood on the five acres, I had bought. I went to the next neighbor's and bought standing timber. I hired a good many hands and chopped the wood and sold it. Sometimes I made as much as forty dollars after paying all my hands, in a week. I took a notion to come to Detroit to attend to some business. I gave up the business to a friend of mine that I thought a great deal of. I liked him so much that I paid his way to Detroit to see the city. He had not been away from home before. He was reared in that place. He left the charge of things to a friend of his, for he expected to be gone two weeks. When the two weeks were almost spent, I went down with him to buy his ticket to go back to Indianapolis again. I told him to take charge of the business, and told him he must figure very close, so as to find out whether he made any thing or not. I told him to write to me often and give me an account of how he was getting along, and I would answer his letters. I told him I would try to start the wood business in Detroit, and if I succeeded, I would want him to come here. We parted, and I went out into the woods to see what prospect there was for me to start business in the wood line, but I found out there was not much show for me in buying timber standing, as most of it was soft wood. I saw that all the hard wood came from Canada, and it was impossible for me to make anything on this side of the river, in the wood line. I was out about four miles from the city, looking around to see what course I should take to get into business. At that time they were enlisting colored soldiers, they had barracks out in the eastern part of the town. While I was out there, a body of patrolmen came along hunting for deserters. They hailed me, and asked me what the reason was I did not enlist, a big able-bodied man like me. I told them I did not care about enlisting. I had been through so much hardship, that I wanted to learn all I could, now that I was in a position where I could learn. They were very angry at me, and told me I had better be down freeing my people. I said to them, yes, I had been planning that, two or three years before the war broke out, and I thought I had given them a great deal of light. He was very angry when I told him that, and said that every colored man ought to take up arms and go into the field. I said to him, yes, I thought so too, if there was any chance of the rebels whipping the Union soldiers. I told him I did not think God intended the devil to gain such a wicked victory. He asked me if I would enlist as a soldier. I said I did not think I would. I told him my mind taught me better, that I thought at some future day I might be of some great benefit. He asked me what benefit I expected to be. I told him I did not know, but I had great hope and trust in the future. He asked me what I was doing out in the woods. I told him I was looking for a spot to start in the wood business. He asked me where I came from. I told him from Indianapolis, Indiana. He asked me how I came to leave there and come here. I told him that I had been here before, and I liked this city better than any place I had been in yet. He told me to fall in the ranks that he suspected I was a bounty jumper. I told him I was not, that I had never enlisted in the army. I did not believe in bounty jumpers, if a man enlisted he ought to fight. He said fall in the ranks, I will take you down to the barracks, I want to try and make a soldier of you. I told him I would go with him for the sake of peace. They brought me down and put me in the guard house waiting for a trial, for what, I did not know. They came in every day to ask me if I would enlist. I told them I would not. I began to study what plan I should adopt to get relief. A dream came to me that I was travelling West, and I came across some strange people, and they took me in. The next day they carried me out to take some exercise. I met Colonel Bond returning from drilling the soldiers. I asked him what they had me in prison for. He said he did not know anything about it, as it had not come before him. I was much encouraged because his face looked so pleasant and just. He said, I will see into your case, and have you brought before me as soon as possible. I said I would be thankful to him if he would release me as soon as he could. He said he would. The next day was Sunday, and in the morning he sent for me to be brought before him. My heart was rejoiced when he sent for me, for my heart felt clear from any wrong to any person. I had it arranged that if anything came up against my character, I could send back to Indianapolis, and get an answer in a very short time by telegraph. I went before the Colonel and stated my case, and he called in the man that arrested me, and he could not bring anything against me, only that he thought I ought to be a soldier. Colonel Bond said he was sorry that I had been kept in the guard-house two weeks for nothing. He asked me to have breakfast before I left. I told him no, that I was so glad to be released that I could not eat anything. He told the guard to pass me out. I felt as though I was free once more. After I came out, my friends asked me how I came to be arrested, that they never knew anything against me. I told them I did not think they were friends, as they never inquired into the matter. I had to plead my own cause. They said they thought I was an upright man. I did not think it was very friendly for them never to inquire after me, or to try and procure my release. I began to wonder what kind of business I should follow, for I saw that I could not make anything at the wood business. After seven days the dream I had in the guard-house came into my mind, about going out West. I took the train for the West that same day, but I did not know what place I would stop at. I was doing as God directed me in a dream. I got to a town called Monroe City, and it seemed to me that was the place. I got off the train there, and wandered around the town, and I came to the conclusion that was not the place for me. I took the plank road West on foot. I traveled till night came on. I was five miles from the city, then I began to look for a stopping place. I inquired of the people I met on the road, whether there was any colored people in the neighborhood. They told me there was not. I began to think where I should find a place to stop, for there was some trouble in finding a place to stop among white people at that time. I went about half a mile farther on, and I came to a house that I thought would suit my purpose. I called at this house, the gentleman was out, but the lady was there. I asked her if I could stay all night. She said, certainly I could. I was much lifted up then. After a while, the

gentleman came in, and the lady told him I wanted to stay
all night. He said it was all right. He asked me which way
thee was going. I was much pleased to hear him say that,
for I knew then that he was a Quaker. I told him I did not
know myself, that I was hunting for work. He said he
wanted to hire a man, and he asked me how much I wanted
a month. I told him I did not know. I told him I thought
they were paying from fourteen to eighteen dollars a
month. He asked me if I knew a man by the name of Carter.
I told him I did. He said that he formerly lived in that
neighborhood. The evening passed off very friendly.
Supper time came, and I knew it was not customary for the
colored people to sit down to the same table with the white,
and I did not know what to do. They called us into supper,
and I began to look for the side table. He asked me to sit
down to the table with him, and it astonished me for him to
ask me to sit down with him, for that was the first time I
had ever sat down and eat with the white folks in my life. I
felt as if I had hit the right spot. I had heard there was a
place where they did not respect color, and I thought I had
found that place at last, after all my traveling. I began
casting my eyes around to see what they all thought about
it, but it looked to me as if I was as much respected as
anyone at the table. I was much pleased and enjoyed myself
well. After supper they asked me where I came from. I told
them I was a Southern man from the Southern States. He
asked me how I liked it in these parts. I told him I liked it
very much. He said I have been wanting to see the bond
people set free, for a long time. He said that time was
coming when all the bond people would be set free, and he
was rejoiced, for it was a great wrong in the land. The time
passed until bed time, and as I was tired from my journey, I
went to bed. The next morning I arose much rested, and

when breakfast time came, we all sat down. After breakfast, the lady got up and took the Bible and commenced looking over it. The gentleman asked me if I had religion. I told no, I had not. The lady commenced to read a chapter in the Bible, and after that, we all kneeled down to pray. The Quaker prayed, and after he was done, his wife prayed. I wondered to myself while they were praying what that amounted to. After the prayer was over, he asked me if I was going to stay with him a month. I said no, I did not think I would, that I was going to travel around and see if I could not do better. He said if you do not get a place before night, come back and stop with me all night. I hunted around from one place to another all day, and I began to think the Quaker's house was surely the place my dream directed me to go. When night came I returned back there again. He asked me if I had found a place. I told him I had not. He told me that I had better stay with him. I told him I thought I would stay with him a white. I stopped with him for a few days, and every morning they would have prayer after breakfast, and that would set my mind to wondering. I did not stay there long, I did not feel exactly well. I left and came back to Detroit. There was a man named Mr. Warsaw, who kept a boarding-house on Cass street, between Jefferson avenue and Larned street, and I went to board with him. I began to study what I had heard when I was at the Quaker's, about being born again and serving the Lord and wishing to do to others as I would be done by, and I studied the matter over very close. I had been hearing such talk as that for some time, but considered it all a humbug, for the people down South would preach about being born again and treating their neighbor as they wanted them to treat him, and they would pray, and call upon God to forgive their sins, and would come home and commence beating and abusing their slaves. I considered it all a humbug. On the other hand, that Quaker took me in, and shared everything with me the same as he had himself, even sit me down to the same table with his family, and that looked as if he was trying to follow the precepts he was teaching to others, and that came into my mind and bothered me much.

I commenced whitewashing around the city again. I whitewashed till harvest time. I started out among the farmers when harvest began, and it came into my mind to go back to that same Quaker again. I stopped with him about two weeks, and he was very glad to see me, and made me welcome. His wife read the Bible to me often, and told me the meaning of what she read. I began to learn many things about the Bible and the salvation of our souls, that I knew nothing about before. This Quaker had two or three brothers living close by, and they all seemed to believe alike. I visited them often, and they received me the same as the first one did. I was much tempted to believe in their principles, and in all of my traveling I had never been taught so much wisdom, and had never seen so much wisdom as I saw among them. It seemed to me that they had great hope from on high; they expected to inherit their Father's Kingdom, which was a cause of great study to me, but I never told them that they had treated me different from what I was accustomed. I acted as if I had received such treatment all my life. I began to talk about going away. He told me he would like to have me stay, but if I would go away, he hoped that the next time he saw me, I would have religion. Then I made up my mind to go back to Indianapolis, for I could do business there better than I could out this way.

I went back to Indianapolis. When I arrived there I found my friend who was in business with me, and asked him how he succeeded in his business. He said well, better than he had ever done in his life before. He asked me if I intended to go into the wood business again. I told him that was my calculation. I asked him if he would go into business with me. He said he was ready at any time. I traveled around and found it hard to buy timber close by the city. I heard of some timber for sale at a place called White River, about nine miles from the city, and I bought nine acres of timber close to the river, and there was a canal near by. I could send the timber down by the boat. I took my friends and went up and put up a cabin and prepared for business. We chopped down the timber and sent it down to the city by the canal boat. We had a little trouble about shipping our wood, for the captain of the canal boat did not want to ship any wood down the river, unless it went through his hands. I carried on the wood business there for about six months, and had good success. I heard there was a great prospect for selling wood at the Missouri River, and I took a notion to go down there. I settled up my business there, and took the cars for St. Louis and arrived there safe, although we were delayed seven hours on account of a freight train having run off the track, and we suffered from hunger, being out on the plains and no town near by. I put up at a hotel there. The landlord asked me where I came from, and I told him Indianapolis, Indiana. He said board here is seven dollars a week. I told him that I was very tired and would like a bed. He took me up to the third story, put me in a room and told me not to lock my door, for if I did I could not unlock it again, and would have to go down on the outside. After he told me that, he went on down stairs. I thought there must be something wrong about what he told me. I locked the door and unlocked it very easy, so that they would not hear me. I thought they were fixing to rob me. I made the door fast and pulled the bed against it, and put some trunks at the foot of the bed so that they could not push the door open if they tried to in the night. I went to bed and began thinking about what he had told me about not locking my door, and lay awake until sometime late in the night, when hearing somebody working at my door and feeling myself safe, I did not pay any attention to them, but lay awake and listened, and after they found that they could not get in, they walked off very light. The next morning I went down, and the landlord asked me how I rested. I told him very well. Breakfast was ready, and I went in to eat. I was watching all his movements then. The time passed off till night. When night came, he had another friend of his to try and find out whether I had any money or not. They had a long talk, and I sat in the room and acted as if I was not paying any attention to them. I thought I understood the whole matter. I was ready for them, and after they had done talking, this man came to me and pretended that he was a great friend to me. After a long conversation, he wanted to know how many times I had jumped the bounty, I told him that I had never jumped the bounty, and I did not believe in it. I thought if a man enlisted, he ought to go on and do according to his promise. He said a great many of the colored men had jumped the bounty, and he thought it was right, and he said he had jumped it seven times himself. I told him I did not think it right, and would not be guilty of it. He asked me if I had ever been in that city before. I told him I did not know many people in St. Louis. He asked me who I knew in the city. I told him it would not do him any good to tell him who I knew. I began to be tired of hearing thieves' talk, and told the landlord I would like to go to bed.

He charged me particularly not to lock my door, for if I did I would have to come down on the outside. I fixed everything the same as the night before. I had not been in bed very long, before I heard them working at my door again, but I paid no attention to them, for I knew they could not get in. A voice called to me in the night and said, "get up and flee from this place." I lay and studied over all things, and I knew that voice was a warning to me to leave that city. When morning came, I got up and put everything back in its place again, and fled from that city.

I went where there was a large settlement of colored people chopping wood, on the Missouri River, and stopped with them for a while, but things did not go to suit me, and I left that place. I looked around then to see what chance there was for doing business in the wood line. I saw my chance was very poor in that part of the country. I left there and went about thirty miles farther on, to another settlement of colored people. I looked around in that neighborhood until I saw there was no chance there to get into the wood business. Then I took the train and went to Jefferson City. I was badly deceived when I got there, it being the capital of Missouri, and such a small city. I walked around and viewed the city, and then went ten miles from Jefferson City across the river, and found the bushwhackers were very bad, and were killing a great many people, and I came back to Jefferson City for safety. I then went two miles from the city and commenced chopping wood at that place. The news came that Abraham Lincoln was killed, and I wept much, knowing that through God's help, he had done much for an oppressed people, and had been the cause of teaching many persons wisdom. Although I knew that Death was our sure portion in this world, I had great hopes in Mr. Johnson, for he claimed to be the colored people's Moses. I found that the Dutch people had a great opinion of Lincoln, though all the rebels were rejoiced. They told me they would get all their slaves back, now that they had got a Southern man for President, and it seemed as if they started afresh in killing people. After that, I could hear of people being killed every other night. The times got so warm there, that I left that place and came back to St. Louis. A man on the train asked me if I was going to stop at St. Louis. I told him I was. He said a friend of his drove a hack, and told me he would carry me to a first-class house. When we got there he took me to his friend's hack. I got in and they kept driving me around until I saw they were taking me out of the city, instead of carrying me to a first-class hotel. I told him to stop and let me out. He stopped, and I opened the door and jumped out. He asked me what I was getting out for. I told him he was taking me out in the country. He told me to get into the hack again. I told him I would not do it. He then asked me how much money I had. I told him it was none of his business how much money I had. He told me he wanted five dollars for driving me farther out of town than I was at the depot. For the sake of peace I gave him a dollar. It was about ten o'clock at night. Then I thought that every time I went to St. Louis I fell into the hands of thieves. Then I told them that when a man hired them to drive him to any part of the city, he ought to do as he was ordered. I believed in everybody doing as near right as he knew how. He drove off and left me, and I was farther from the place I wanted to go, than before I left the depot. I found a place, stopped all night and took breakfast, and went down to the cars and left the city. I went twenty-three miles from St. Louis, near St. Charles, and there I fell in with a man who wanted sixty thousand rails made. I asked him what wages he paid. He said a dollar and a half a hundred. I knew I could make money at that price, for it was the best of cotton wood timber. I commenced making rails for him, and I generally split about twelve hundred rails a week. There was a great many in the same business and the job soon ran out. I began thinking about the Quaker I stopped with in Michigan, and what he had told me about the Bible, and about being born again. I thought I would try and find out what it was to be born again in the Spirit of God. I fasted and prayed that I might be born of the Spirit of God, and might have treasures laid up in heaven. There were about thirty colored people in the woods, and they had a great many cabins built. While I was trying to be born again by the Spirit of God, a Catholic priest came riding through the woods, and asked the colored people if they would allow him to preach to them. He told them he had come all the way from the old country to save sinners, and if he could save one sinner, he would be satisfied. They sent for him to come and preach to them. That was about the middle of the week. He sent word that he would be there about eleven o'clock on Sunday. When he came, there was a colored man preaching, and he stood out of doors until he got through. Then the priest came in and began, making the sign of the Cross, and he took a text the same as any other preacher. He got through with his sermon, and told the people he would be there again next Sunday.

When Sunday came again, he came as he promised to. When he began to preach, he told the colored people that the Catholic church was the only one that was right, and that all other churches were wrong. When he had finished preaching, he told them that he would come the next Sunday. The people were disgusted with his preaching, and

did not want him to come back again. When he came back
again the next Sunday, a colored man was preaching. After
the colored man had concluded his sermon, he came in and
asked the colored man if he could swear that was the Bible,
and the people then asked the priest if he could swear the
book he had in his hand was the Bible. He said yes, he
could, that it was in Latin, and that preachers ought always
to preach in Latin when they preached right. The colored
people told him it would do very well to preach in Latin in
a country where they understood Latin, and knew what he
was talking about, and one colored man told him if he
preached in Latin in this country, he would not be the cause
of many people turning to God. The priest said nobody
could be saved only through the priest. The colored people
told him that they did not want to hear any more of his
preaching. The priest took up his hat, and when he was out
of doors, he told them they were all going down to hell, and
he was very sorry that he could not save any of them. That
was the last of his preaching to the colored people in that
part of the country.

I was almost through with the rail business and harvest
was commencing. Then I hired myself to a man that had a
large field of wheat. I worked for him, but he was a strong
rebel, and he had been in the Rebel army. While I was
working for him, I received a new spirit, and then I knew
what it was to be born again in the Spirit of God. I spent the
happiest two weeks I ever experienced in my whole life, for
the Spirit of God was dwelling in me. After that I felt as it I
had no friends in this world, and I tried to retain that spirit I
had received from on high, but I felt as if it had left me. I
knew the Spirit of God did dwell in me for two weeks, for I
felt a happiness that I knew was given to me from the Lord,

and when I felt so lonely in heart, I began to fast and pray
to the Lord again, but it seemed as if everything I put my
hand to turned against me, and I wept much, and I cried
unto the Lord and asked him what I should do to keep his
spirit which I had received once, and I heard the sound of a
voice, and it seemed to me as if it was a long way off, and
it said, go and tarry, and I wept much. This voice followed
me from one day to another, till I felt sorry and low in spirit
and humble to the Lord my Maker, and the spirit within my
heart told me to go back to the Quaker's. I told the spirit
that I did not wish to go, for the Quaker and his family
were highly educated people, and I was ignorant. This spirit
kept urging me from one day to another. I would talk to the
spirit, and say if I went back to the Quaker's and told them I
had received the spirit, they would be sure to call upon me
to pray, and as they were learned and I was ignorant, I did
not want to go back. The spirit said he had the truth and the
light, and he will bear with you. After all of that, I still
fought against going back, and everything I set my heart
upon after that, I failed in. I had great ideas but could do
nothing, for I was wrestling against the Spirit of God. I was
determined not to go back to the Quaker's. I took the train
for Indianapolis, Indiana, and thought I would spend the
winter there. I went to that city and stopped, and went
around to see my friends. I stayed there about two weeks,
but that same spirit followed me, and I saw no satisfaction.
I was determined to stay there that winter, and I went out
and prepared everything to stop all winter. At the end of
two weeks, my mind became so troubled that I could not
rest, but the Lord shewed me his grace was sufficient for all
things. I took the train for Toledo. I landed there, and
thought I would spend the winter in Toledo. I found out
that the spirit troubled me more than in all the other places.

I made up my mind to go back to the Quaker's, and when I was started on the road, the spirit told me that I must not hire myself to him by the month, but to go there and stop, not saying anything to him about hiring me, and nothing about money. I went and done just as the spirit directed me, and when I arrived at the Quaker's house he was very glad to see me, and asked me how I had been since I left him. I told him I had been well. Then he asked me if I had professed religion. I told him no, I had not. I was afraid if I said yes, be would call upon me to pray. He told me that he had hoped I would have religion when I saw him again. He asked me if I was going to stay with him. I told him I thought I would stop with him. He asked me how much I wanted a month. I told him nothing, for the spirit directed me to come and stay with him, and not take any money. He asked me what the spirit told me to do when I got to his house. I knew what the spirit had told me, that he had the truth and the light, and that he would bear with me. I did not tell the Quaker what the spirit had said. I kept that secret from him to this day. I went on to tell him how I could not see any rest in Missouri, that I was directed to come to his house, but I did not wish to come, and I went to Indianapolis, Indiana, but I could see no peace there, and that I was directed to come to his house. I told him that I took the train and went to Toledo, and thought I would not go out to his house, and I told him I was more troubled there than any place I had been yet, and I made up my mind that I would yield. He told when God's Spirit took hold of anybody, he troubled their minds till they were willing to obey him. He told me to look to God for strength. He said that he grew stronger in the faith every day, and that it was good to wait on the Lord. He said whoever waited on the Lord would have great treasures in heaven. Then I felt as if

I had done God's will, I had come to the spot He had directed me to, and I felt happy and rejoiced. I thought that I had no more to do. I thought I would stay there until the spirit directed me to go farther on. They had prayers every morning that the Lord sent around, and I did not think it was as much of a humbug as I had been thinking it. I felt it was all right, and I saw it was good to have the grace of God dwelling in our hearts. I saw it kept a great deal of evil away; I saw it was good to take a drink from the running spring, for it caused life everlasting to spring up in my heart. I could see the good of praying from one day to another, and both the Quaker and his wife would talk to me, and tell me what I had to do, so as to be able to inherit the Kingdom of Heaven. He asked me often about the spirit directing me back there, but I told him the same as I did the first time he asked me.

He had a brother who live nearby, and he also drank from the spring of life every morning, and I was telling him that I was directed to come back to John Atkinson, and I asked him what he thought about it. He told me the light in which he looked at it was, for him to give me good instruction. I made myself easy, but I had my own opinion, because I knew I had tasted the Lamb of Jesus, and I knew there was wisdom all the way through, and a good understanding. His brother asked me if I had experienced religion. I told him no. My mind was sorely grieved because I had denied the spirit. The spirit spoke openly to me and said "let your light shine." I told the spirit that they were learned people, and I could not make my light shine, and the spirit said, "my grace is sufficient for all things." But I still rebelled against God, and for seven days I could neither eat or drink, and it seemed that when I had eaten one or two mouthfuls I was filled up. The spirit said to me again, "let your light shine," and I wept much, because I knew the Quakers were talented compared to me. One morning the lady, as she was getting up from prayer, looked at me very pleasant and said, why do you not pray for the good of your soul. I told her because I have not professed religion. She said, why do you not pray to the Lord to forgive you, that you may be born of the spirit. I gave her no answer, but the Spirit of God was dwelling in my heart. One morning I could eat only a few mouthfuls of breakfast, and the lady took the Bible and read a chapter, and then we all kneeled down to pray, and the spirit worked within me mightily, and I strove against it, but it seemed as if I broke out in prayer, and the Lord put words in my mouth to speak. I was happy, and felt happy all day. My mind was relieved, for I had carried out the Lord's will. From that day out, I learned wisdom and understanding. After that, I could join them in their morning prayers, and I saw that praying in the morning was a light that shone before you all day, and the cause of keeping much evil away. One night after I had gone to bed the spirit spoke to me and said, "be strong in faith." There was a large tree standing in one corner of the lane, and the spirit told me that if my faith was strong enough I could move yonder tree, it said if my faith was strong enough, I could say to the tree, hence away, and it would obey me. I was much grieved at what I heard, for I did not understand it. The spirit taught me that I could learn of him every day, till I grew mighty in him, and that nothing was impossible with him. I felt that I had more to learn from the spirit, but I would have to learn it through much fasting and prayer. From that day to this, I believe God will dwell with people in this land, if they only practice that, and I always will believe it till I carry this out. I went to church, and I was in the habit of getting up and speaking in the class, but I could only say a few word, for my heart was full, and I felt in my heart that there would be a day I could explain myself better than I could then. Many times I would not go to class-meeting, because I could not speak as well as I desired to, but I fully believed the day would come when I would be able to say all I desired to, and see as clear as a crystal.

I often went to his brother's house and joined him in prayer, and felt that I was doing the Lord's will. I stayed with the Quaker nearly seven months, and the lady tried to learn me to spell. I learned some, but my mind was so taken up in the Lord's cause, I did not learn much. She learned me how to write my name, and I felt proud over that. When the seven months were almost gone, I felt my time was nearly out in staying there, and I felt released. I asked him for twenty dollars, and he gave it to me willingly, and would have given me more if I wanted it.

I took the cars to Detroit, for the spring was opening, and stopped again with my friend Warsaw, and I went into the whitewashing business again. I had very good success, and the Spirit of God was with me and I was happy. When the rush was over, business began to get dull, and I went to Oberlin, Ohio, to see that part of the world, and I was much pleased at the good laws they had at Oberlin, and marked it out that if I ever was able, I would go there and go to school. Then I went seven miles from Oberlin and went to work in a brick yard, and when harvest began, I left there and went into the harvest field, and I stayed there until the harvest was over. I took the train for Columbus, Ohio, and stopped there two weeks, and had a very good time, because the spirit was with me. I went from there to Yellow Springs, Ohio. I had heard so much talk about the Springs that I wanted to see them, and enjoyed myself very much there, and thought over what great things the Lord had given to the people to enjoy themselves and benefit their bodies. I went from there to Xenia, Ohio, and I stayed there a few days, and went from there to Harvestborough, and went three miles from that place and commenced to chop wood. I chopped for about three months, and enjoyed myself all the time I was there. Sometimes I would feel high in the spirit. I went from there to Franklin, the water had been very high and overflowed the corn fields. I got a job of husking corn, and worked there about three weeks. I took a notion to start back to Detroit, and while on the way, my mind told me to go back and see the Quaker's. I called by and stopped with them three days, and they were glad to see me. After the three days were spent, I went to Monroe City, and took the cars for Detroit, and went back to my old boarding-house on Cass street. I stopped in this city a few days and found my friends all well. My spirit directed me to go to Jackson, and I stopped there a week, and after that went to Lester, and went three miles, out in the country, and got a job of chopping wood. I built a cabin for the winter, and chopped there alone all winter. I had the cabin to myself, nobody being in the woods but me, and the Spirit of God dwelt with me while I was out there by myself in the woods. The spirit told me to hold out faithful and riches would be added to me. While I was out there by myself, I was taken very sick, and was sick for some time. The spirit told me one night if I had faith my sickness would be removed from me. I was so sick I could not get up and down in the bed. I lost all hope of earthly things. Then I began to put strong trust in God, believing he could sit me up straight. I prayed to God to remove this sickness from my flesh, and that I might have my health again, and I felt it move, I felt as if cold water had been poured over me, and arose in good health and thanked God for it. I saw it was good to wait on the Lord, and I saw he was ready to help them when they were in need, but it takes strong faith to carry this out, and no hopes in this world. After thinking how the Lord had removed my sickness, I thought I would take a new step in this world. The spirit taught me to look for a companion. Then I began to think if in any of my travels I had seen anybody that I thought would suit me, and I had not come across the right person yet. Then I began to think what benefit a wife would be to me, and I thought she would be a true friend, for I had nobody I could call a true friend. I thought again it would be the means of my having a home, and be the cause of my settling down, and be the cause of settling my mind on one certain thing, and I thought it would be the means of my prospering in the future. After that I thought all these things over and examined them well, and thought it was good, and when I was done thinking over this matter, it was ten o'clock at night, and I went to bed, and after I went to sleep I dreamed that I saw a woman standing before me, and that she came from a strange country, and thought she suited my taste, and I said that is the woman I am going to marry. When I awoke in the morning, behold it was nothing but a dream. I made up my mind that I would see that woman before long. The day passed away, and I had been thinking about my dream all through the day, and was going to settle up my wood business in the country about that time. When night came, I was counting up what my job of wood cutting would come to until bed time, and then went to bed. I dreamed that night about three yellow snakes, and I thought the smallest one of the three was trying to bite me, and I thought that one of the other snakes got between me and the one that was trying to bite me, and I thought the largest one of all stood and looked on at the other two. I thought the first two snakes came in contact and fought awful, and I thought the one that was taking up for me whipped the other one badly, and I thought the largest one that had been looking on parted the two that were fighting. I thought the one that got whipped crawled off and the other two followed him, and I thought I went on after them. The largest one of all told the other two snakes that they had better make friends and say no more about it. And the smallest one said he would tell it, for I would be sure to tell it, and he would tell it himself. I thought the largest one told me not tell. I said to the smallest one, if they would make friends and settle the matter, I would leave that place. He agreed to settle it and they all made friends, and I thought I left the place. After I awoke I studied that dream over. I always knew that if you dreamed about a snake, it was a sure sign some one had ill will against you. I did not think anyone out there had any ill will against me, for they always said I was a pious man, for nobody but a pious man could live in the woods alone as I did. When day break came, I got up and had everything ready, because they were coming to measure the wood I had chopped through the winter, that morning, so that I could leave. They came about nine o'clock and commenced measuring the wood. There were three men, and I thought two of those men were great friends of mine, but the other one I did not think was friendly to me. I knew nothing against him, but I thought he was not my friend. They measured my wood, and after they had measured it, the smallest one that I took to be the best

friend of the three, did not want to pay me. The one I
thought did not like me, asked him the reason he would not
pay me as he had agreed to. He told the smallest one he
must pay me, if he did not he could do the other thing.
Then they came in contact with each other and had a very
bloody fight and the other man and myself stood and
looked at them. He cried out enough, and the largest man
parted them, and the man that had been whipped went away
and we followed him. Then the large man told him to settle
the matter among ourselves, and not to let the family or any
of the neighbors know anything about it, but the little one
said I would tell it, and he might as well tell it himself. I
told him if he would pay me, I would take the train and
leave the place. Then he paid me and I came away. This
happened about five years ago. I did not think of the dream
I had about the three yellow snakes at the time. I stopped in
Jackson all night, and after I went to bed, the matter came
before my mind, and just as I had dreamed about the three
snakes, it all happened. Then I thought about the dream I
had about the woman, and felt sure that dream would be
fulfilled at some future time. The next morning I took the
train for Detroit, and went to my boarding-house on Cass
street. They appeared very glad to see me again, and took
up my old trade of whitewashing. Business was good and I
had very good success, and spent many happy days. As I
went from one house to another, the spirit was with me.
The time passed away. In my going around I came across
the woman I had seen in my dream. I examined my mind,
and knew she was the woman I had seen in my dream, and
kept my eyes on her for about two months before I made
myself acquainted with her. Through an acquaintance, I
made myself known to her. After becoming acquainted I
was much pleased with her company and passed off the

evening very sociably. I had the pleasure of being in her company a few more evenings, and we met from time to time, until finally we were engaged to be married. I took the notion to go out to the Eastern States and through Canada. I took the train to Toronto, and from there to Montreal, and took the train and went from there to Pond City, Vermont. When I was on the way to Vermont, I inquired whether there were any colored people living there. They told me that no colored people lived in the city. I thought I was about trumped on account of the difficulty in colored people stopping at the hotel with white people. When I arrived in town, I found there was no difficulty in getting a hotel to stop at, and enjoyed myself well while stopping there, but it was not as fine a city as I expected. I saw more hills there than I had seen for quite a while, and the greater portion of the people I talked with were French, but they appeared to be very sociable. I went from there to Portland, Maine, but did not stay there long, what little I saw of the city I liked very much, and went from there to Boston, Massachusetts. I was much pleased when I landed there, having often heard that Boston was in a State greatly in favor of colored people. I chatted with a great many of the old people there, and they were all in favor of the colored people, and it pleased me much. I thought of going out into the country, for it was nearly harvest time. I walked about six miles, and came to a very fine house, and thought that would be my place to inquire for work. I asked the gentleman if he wanted to hire a man. He said no, that he had just hired a man, but a friend of mine wants to hire a man, he lives about a mile from here. He walked over with me to show me the place. I thought it very strange that a rich man like him, should take so much trouble with me, as to take me to a neighbor to try and find a place for me to work. The gentleman's name was Hickey, where he took me. He hired me while harvest lasted, and he asked me how much I wanted a day. I said two dollars. He told me he had worked all day long for six shillings. I told him there was a difference between that day and these times, people worked for money now. He told me to go to work, and if I earned it he would pay me. Then I wrote back to Detroit to the lady I was engaged to marry, for I was anxious to hear from her, and received an answer in seven days from the time I had written.

Sunday came and they were afraid it was going to rain, and they wanted to pile the hay in cocks on Sunday. I told him I could not pile any hay on Sunday, I did not think it was right to work on that day, and his two sons and myself had a great argument, whether it was right to work on Sunday or not. They partly agreed with my views. I told them I never expected to work on Sunday in the fields. I had a good time with these people, and stayed with them till after harvest, which lasted thirty-three days; I visited the city often, and walked around and looked at all the different things to be seen. I saw a great many Commons in the city, which surprised me, for I thought such a large city would be built up. I looked at the Monument, and went to see the navy yard at Charlestown.

When the harvest was over, the man I worked for paid me at the rate of two dollars a day, and it seemed as if the people had taken a great liking to me, and did not wish to have me go away. I receive a letter from my lady every week. I stayed a week with them after I had finished working for them. I was thinking what I would do next, and made up my mind to go to Webster, forty-five miles from

Boston. When I arrived there I began to look for work. I went to a very large foundry and asked them if they would like to hire a man. He told me there was no vacant place at present, but to look around and if I could not find any one that wanted to hire, to come back to him and he would give me work. Being Saturday, I went to another man, and he said he had no vacant place, but if I did not find a place before night, to come back to him and he would give me some work. I left word that if he heard any person inquiring for a man to work, to send them to the boarding house where I was stopping. A gentleman in a buggy drove around to the place where I was stopping, and inquired for me. He told me he had a farm two miles from Clappville, and asked me if I would go out to his place to work, and how much I wanted a day. I told him that I wanted a dollar and a half a day. I worked for him two weeks, visited around in the neighborhood, and found the people quite sociable. I thought the State of Massachusetts was the finest place I had ever been in. While I was there I received several letters from my lady, which cheered up my spirits. After I was done working for that man, I thought I would go to Springfield.

I went from there to Albany in the State of New York, and took the train from there to Niagara Fall, and looked at all the things worth seeing there, and then took the cars for Detroit. I arrived here safe, without a day's sickness while I was gone, and went back to my old boarding-house on Cass street. I sat down and studied over all my travels, and I saw the lady I was engaged to marry, and we were much rejoiced to meet one another. I thought since I had got free from men and traveled far and near, I saw there was a great evil in the land. I did not understand before, and wondered in my mind that as many preachers as the Lord had called to preach, I wondered they had not built up a better light than I had seen. I took another view of the South. There I saw a great many men that said the Lord had called them to preach, and at the same time they owned a great many slaves. I thought that the Lord surely could not have called them, or they would have given freedom to their slaves. I thought that matter over, and saw how many churches they had built all over the Southern States, and so much evil going on, it made my heart tremble to think what wickedness was going on, and it seemed to me, that instead of the righteous dwelling in the churches, the devil had the bill of sale of them. I thought that a new light would shine on this earth to show people different from what they had been doing, and I commenced looking at myself, knowing that I was living in an evil land and liable to be lost on the wayside, and prayed to God to strengthen me with his Holy Spirit, so that I would be able to resist the temptations of this wicked world. I wished I was able, through the Spirit of God, to show some light in this world for the salvation of souls; although I thought I was advancing in age, and would not be able to give any light myself. I thought I would marry and raise a son, and I prayed that he would be full of the Holy Ghost. I was married on the 20th October, 1867, and lived on the corner of Cass and Larned streets. We lived very happy, and I enjoyed myself better than when I was traveling from one place to another. Everything passed off very favorable. In the course of time, the Lord blessed me with a son, and I thought then I would accomplish my aim, and I was much rejoiced, but he only lived to be nine months and three weeks old, and then he died. I was very much grieved, and I prayed to the Lord that he would bless me with another son, and in the course of another year, we had another son, and I was very much rejoiced to think the Lord had answered my prayers, but my joy was soon turned to grief, for he only lived to be two weeks and two days old. Then I studied the matter over and left it in the Lord's hands to do with me as he pleased, and I would be guided by him in all things. One night I had a dream, I thought I was carried up on a high pillar, and I thought I saw four pools of water, and I saw a man standing by me, and he said come up a little higher, and he asked me if I saw those four pools of water. I told him I did, and he said I will tell you the meaning of those four pools of water. He said those four pools of water were kingdoms, and he pointed down to one kingdom, (he picked it out from all the rest), and said that kingdom was richer than all the rest, and said it was able to buy kingdoms to go with it. And one kingdom stood off by itself, and a great jealousy arose against it in the other kingdoms, because it grew so powerful. Then the man told me to look down, and I thought I saw the sea, and thought it looked blue, and I thought that all kinds of boats and fleets you could mention were in the sea. I thought I saw a great army, and I thought that great army was going against that kingdom that had grown so strong. I thought there was a very strong fort at one end of the kingdom, but the great army went around the fort and entered the city, and I heard a voice sound in the city, saying, "woe, woe, to thy happiness." I awoke, and found it was all a dream.

I carried on my business in the city, and in the course of another year the Lord blessed us with a daughter. I thought my calculations about raising up a son were broken up, although I am very well pleased with my daughter. She is seven months old, and has hardly had a day's sickness. I recalled to my mind the time when my wife went down home to Toronto, Canada, to see her mother, and being a man that was in the habit of always coming home as soon as my work was done, both before and since I was married, my wife being gone, the evenings seemed so long and lonesome, and having heard so much about what good times the people were having at balls, tea parties and festivals, I thought I would go out and see for myself what was going on. I heard there was a first-class ball to be given at Funke's Hall, and I made up my mind to go and look on, just to satisfy my mind on that subject. I looked on, but could not see any pleasure people could derive from it. I thought it looked more like heathens than a civilized people living in an enlightened country. The thought came into my mind that amusements of that kind done very well down south, when we did not know any better, but in this country, I thought they had better be home spending the evening some other way, but it appeared as if the company collected there enjoyed themselves very much, and I thought it was the cause of many persons young and old straying from the right path.

There is another thing I often study since I obtained my freedom, and wonder how so much wickedness was carried on down South, in what was called a civilized land, and another thing I wondered at is, that the preachers did proclaim from the pulpit that it was right to have slaves, and then said the Lord called them to preach. I often attacked highly educated preachers just to hear what they would say on that point. A great many of them said that was the law of the land, and whatever laws were made, the people must abide by them. I asked them which would be the most profitable at the end of time, to do to your neighbor as you would wish to be done by, or to follow the evil ways of the land. Then he said slavery had become so strong in the land that people had to bear with it. Then I asked him if a man killed another man in an unjust cause, if he would uphold him in doing it. He said no, he would not uphold such a case as that. Then I asked him how he came to uphold slavery. He returned me no answer to that question. I asked him if he thought it was right to drive colored people like cattle, and sell one in this place and some in another place along the road, as they went, and never let them learn in the book. He would not answer me on that matter. We parted from each other, and I attacked other preachers and they said they knew it was wrong, but they dare not preach it, they said it would make hard feelings and anger. I told them if ever God called me to preach, I would tell the truth, I did not care whether they took it or not, so long as I had God to back me. I talked with other preachers, and they said they knew it was not right, and that they had preached it in the pulpit that it would be a curse against them, and that softened my heart, and I thought he studied his neighbor's interests as well as his own. I felt that he had the true knowledge of God, and I felt in my mind that God was teaching him, that he was not going by the laws of the land, and laws that proud and weak-minded people made. I told him no Northern man could travel in the Southern States and speak his own mind, even his own color could not. He said yes, he knew that was a great evil, that people called this country free, but they were mistaken in that. I watched my chance to attack what the people called the Abolitionists, and I took a great liking to talk to them. I found that they all talked the one thing, I found they had no proud heart for themselves, but had kindly feelings for other people. I liked to talk with the

Quakers, I found them a true-hearted people, and they all spoke alike, they did not differ one from the other, they believed in all men being free before the Lord, and it rejoiced my heart to talk with them and hear their opinion and I took a great delight in talking with people to find out what was their ideas about things, whether they were true-hearted or not.

Next I draw your attention to a newspaper I was much mistaken in about the time Lincoln issued his proclamation to the Rebels to law down their arms, if they did not he would free the slaves. I was on the cars coming here, and I heard them talking about Lincoln's proclamation, and I made up my mind to get a paper when I arrived at Detroit. When I got here I put up at the North Star House. The next morning the boy came along with a paper called the Free Press. I had never bought a paper before in my life, and concluded to buy a paper that morning. I bought the Free Press, and hired a boy to read it to me, and the boy read it to me. I thought it was the most curious free paper I ever heard read. It seemed to me that it sided with the rebels, and being in a free State, I was surprised. I could not understand it. I thought the boy had made a mistake in reading it. I thought surely it must be a friend to the colored people, being named the Free Press. The next morning the boy brought around the Free Press again, and I thought I would buy it again. I hired another boy to read it to me, and told him to read about the colored people, but it talked so bitter against them that I could not understand it, yet I was not satisfied about the paper. I thought the boy had not read the paper right, for I thought by the name of the paper it must be a friend to the colored people. I thought I would buy another one next morning. That one I took to a lady, and asked her to read it to me so that I could understand it. I told her to read about the colored people. She read the paper to me, and after she had finished reading it, I asked her to tell me something about that paper, that I thought it was a paper that wanted everybody to be free. She told me it was not in favor of the colored people being free, and from that day to this, I have often wondered how it came to take such a glorious name, when it was so bitterly opposed to the colored people having their freedom, and wondered how an educated nation could be so opposed to an oppressed and ignorant people, when they were the cause of our being in this new land. I often thought it would take better views of the matter than it had done, because it makes dissatisfaction and hard feelings in the country when there is no necessity for it, brings mobs and violence on a weak class of people, when there is no need of it, and if they measure such as that out to the colored people, it will be measured back to them again, and I hope hereafter they will take a more religious view of the matter.

There is another subject I have often studied over, and that is, how the colored people could get along in this country, being shut out of all public business. The best chance I can see that they have of making anything is, when the boats are running. Another thing they never felt safe here until the war broke out, and that is one thing that has kept them behind as long as they have been, but a good spirit entered into the hearts of men, causing them to give equal rights to all men, and that holds up the colored people these days. It removed a certain prejudice from the minds of the people, it gave happiness to their minds, removed hard feelings, and it causes them to look at things in a different light, and gave them a chance to speak their

79

opinion in the land, and if they are only faithful, they will reap the benefit of that law.

Another matter I have often thought about this question, that has arisen in the land, with respect to women voting. I myself am opposed to it, I cannot see where it would be any benefit to them in any way at all. If I could see any benefit it would be to the land, I would be in favor of it. I have talked with a great many learned men, and asked them if they were in favor of it, and they said a woman that has no husband had just as much tax to pay as if she was a man, and they said they thought she ought to vote. I told them if that was all the reason they could give, it could be mended very easily without voting, because where a woman has property, they always marry as soon as time will let them. They told me that they could hold office and do business like a man. I told them I did not think any man would like to have his wife exposed to all kinds of abuse, and did not think any lady would want to vote. Then they said they had just as good a right to vote as the colored people had. Then I told them no person ought to wish to do anything through evil. I told them a man ought always to think before he speaks. I told them that was the cause of so much evil being in the land. I told them I thought it would be one of the greatest evils that could befall the land, if the women should be allowed to vote. I talked with a great many that were opposed to it, and I thought to myself they were about right on that subject.

There is another subject I have studied about. I often thought God sent a messenger through Fremont, at the time he ran for President, and by his running, it gave the idea of freedom to the colored people, it made them think that better times were coming, and the light kept growing for the next four years, and we were perfectly satisfied that the prayers of the slaves had reached up to the Throne of God, and he was angry at the cruelty that was going on in the land, and the Lord intended through Fremont, to liberate the colored people from their cruel bondage. The Lord showed them that they must be watchful and put their trust in Him. The colored people understood who was their friend, but they were looking for the next four years, all over the Southern States, for the great promises the Lord had made to them through Fremont running for President, though he was defeated, he left a light behind that every person understood. I have often studied to myself how great is the wisdom of the Lord. He did not intend that Fremont should be elected, for that would have left the colored people in darkness, and they would not have known which side to take, but by Fremont being defeated, it left the colored people four years more to become enlightened in the great work that was going on for their benefit in this land. I often thought, when they turn out and celebrate the day they received equal rights, they ought never to forget Fremont, because I think he was a great benefactor to the colored people, and shewed them a great light that will never be forgotten. I also often thought that the Lord had shown to John Brown that many should fall on the battle field on account of the light Fremont had shown to the colored people. I often thought the Lord had sent a messenger through John Brown, that he might open the light to the white people, that it might be the cause of their taking a better view of slavery, and that they might use some measure toward breaking it up; but before he accomplished much he was overtaken and hanged. I often thought how hard it was to take a man's life for telling

81

people that slavery was coming to an end. I have no doubt in my mind that a great many people throughout the land wished to keep a class in ignorance in this enlightened age. I often thought that as good a man as Lincoln was that while many failed, he stood through it all and carried his glorious point. He had many to fight against and contend with, but for all that, he carried the glorious point over all.

The day Lincoln was elected President, a great shout of joy went up all through the South, to think that the Lord had answered the prayers that had been uttered all their lives, and many old people rejoiced to think they had lived to see that great day. It seemed as if the slaves understood what was going to happen better than the white people did, because the slaves would walk miles to tell one another what they had heard, and enjoy it. Though John Brown was put to death, he will never be forgotten by the colored people. The rebels thought when they took his life that they would regain all they had lost, but by spilling his blood they only confirmed it, for it put an end to slavery, and it can never be restored.

Andrew Johnson took Lincoln's place because Lincoln was killed before his term expired. I had great hopes in Andrew Johnson, as he pretended to be such a friend to the colored people that they called him Moses. I was looking for some great work he would do for the benefit of an ignorant race, and I kept on the lookout for what Johnson was going to do for us, for I knew we had not received all our rights, and I thought that the Lord had left it in Andrew Johnson's hands to finish the work that Lincoln had begun; but every bill that came up for the benefit of the colored people, Andrew Johnson was the man to throw all the evil on it he could. Then I began to think that he was not quite as good a Moses as I thought he was, still I had some hope that he would do something for an oppressed race, for I thought there must be some good in him. When the bill came up to give the colored people some land to help them along, he vetoed it. He was a man that did a great deal of talking, but he did no good for an ignorant race. He carried his point by saying that people who came from the old country got along and the colored people could do the same. That satisfied me there was no good in Andrew Johnson when he began to compare an educated people with an ignorant class. The people that came from the old country were educated, and had always been free, and to think that they should be compared with colored people that had no education and knew nothing but what wisdom had taught them, made my heart tremble to think an educated man would advance such doctrines. It made me weep, and I studied the matter over at that time, and I thought if he would give the people over fifty years of age the land, I would think there was some good in the South, but he refused them all, and gave them nothing, even after they had labored years and years under cruel treatment, and shut out of all the happiness of the world; and all the light of the world, and I think they have undergone more than any other race that exists, even more than the Indians, because the Indians are paid for their lands every year. The colored people were forced to come here and made to work, and were then turned loose without giving them anything for their labor. It was in the power of the man that helped carry on this cruel treatment, to give us something for our labor, but they turned us loose without giving us anything to help us to get a liviug. Andrew Johnson never did the colored people any good, and I hope he will think of himself and not let the devil cheat him out of his soul. After all of that we are passing along through the world without a home and no money, and no education, but the hopes we had in God bore us up that we would get our rights at a future day. It seems as if one class of people are trying to keep the wisdom and light of the world from us, and are opposed to us. Andrew Johnson threw it back on the States to give us equal rights, and it seemed to me that he threw all the evil he could, in order that the States might throw all the evil they could, that we might be shut out and kept in ignorance. The States did carry out their evil points and kept us in ignorance of the wisdom and light of this world; but I had a hope in the future, for I saw a great many had the light and the wisdom and wanted to share it with the colored people, and that bore my mind up. It went back to Congress to see what they would do for an ignorant class of people, and by Grant being a friend to all nations, he put the bill in the Legislature of every State to act upon it, because he knew there was a good spirit in the Legislatures, and he knew that the bill would pass, for through the legislatures and the good will of God, he stood at the head of the States. The evil followed along after it and threw all the evil light they could upon it. In some of the States the light shown so bright the evil flew off, but it availed nothing, for the evil was there when they started. They passed it on in the other States and even followed it in the Chamber, but it was drive out of the Chamber, and the light shown bright in the land, and the evil took wings and flew through the land, trying to stir up the evil passions of people in order that when election came, the evil might shut many out. It did abridge it many places. Wisdom and light followed after it and tore down the evil places that they had built up in order to carry their point. Today, through a hard struggle, the light is laid open to us that we may enjoy all the privileges of other men, that we might grow strong and understand the wisdom of God, who made all men equal.

The question arises how we got this so soon. It was done by men that had wisdom for others as well as themselves, especially for a down-trodden and ignorant race; while others only built themselves up and never shared with others. I will liken the Republicans to the wise man that built his house on a rock, and the storm and the sea beat against it, it still stands; their light still shines, and every year grows brighter. The Democrats I will liken to the foolish man that built his house on the sand, and the storm and waves beat against it and great was the fall of that house. In the course of every year the Democrats grow weaker, and they will finally die out and be forgotten. The Republicans acknowledge their faults, while the others do not to this day. They say it was wrong to take the rebels' property, but after all, the schools are thrown open to every human being in the land. I have been cheated of all learning, but I hope to get my education so that I will have more light in regard to earthly things, in order that God will throw more light in my mind on heavenly things. I have often thought it was a glorious thing that the Bible is read in the public schools. I think it should remain a law, for it is the cause of keeping much evil out of the land.

I have often thought what a glorious man Grant has been to the country since he has been at the head of the government. He has done all the good possible for an ignorant class of people. When the rebels went to Grant and told him the colored people would not work, he told them to pay them and they would work. He was not like Andrew

Johnson, who did a great deal of talking and kept a great excitement in the country, stirring up evil. Grant talks little, but works for the salvation of the land. My earnest wish is for Grant's re-election, and I think the colored people are built up in Grant for our next President. All the Republicans among the white people I have talked to are greatly in favor of Grant, but the Democrats say the Republicans are going to split. My hope is that no split will occur, and but one man be nominated. The Democrats say they will not make a nomination, but let the Republicans nominate two. I think in cannot work. At the last campaign I visited the Democratic meetings to see if they had any good feeling for the colored people, but I heard nothing but evil. That was the ground they took to abuse the Republican party. The Democratic speakers said the colored people were uncivilized. I thought if so, it would be better to help them, and not to abuse them. I asked some why they talked so, and I was told it was for policy. I said I did not think it policy to take an ignorant and weak class of people, and to try and carry their point by trying to keep them in ignorance, and that did not look like good policy in my view. I attended the Republican meetings and enjoyed it. I did not see any evil they were throwing in the path of the colored people, but instead of throwing evil, they were trying to remove it from their path, and everything went on smooth and nice. I learned many things I did not know before, I enjoyed their meetings, and I heard Speaker Colfax speak. I was much lifted up because he spoke as if he meant what he said, and aimed to carry out what he advocated. They carried all their points, and elected Grant for our President, and I hope the Republicans will be successful again, and elect Grant for the next four years as our President, although they will have many things to fight

against, but they are so well up to it, I know they will fill all
the corners they unlock, and give their hearers satisfaction.
I do not know whether Grant will be nominated President
or not, but if he is not, I hope whoever is, will be elected,
but my solemn wish is, that Grant may be elected, that is if
the Lord spares him. There is another thing Grant had in
view, that I was much pleased with, and that was in making
a friendly treaty with the Island of San Domingo, because I
thought that would be one of the greatest blessings that ever
happened to the colored people, it would have made great
friendship. There being so many colored people in the
United States, it would have created a great friendship
between the colored people here and the people on that
Island in the course of time, and the colored people would
have had a country to travel to in friendship, they would
have understood each other, but the way it is now, we have
no transactions with foreign nations, that we can
understand. It would have been the means of building them
up more substantially than they are now. I had great hopes
when he sent out Commissioners to examine the country,
through I knew they had stolen them from Africa, I hoped
they were going to restore their rights to them again, and
give them a better understanding, that they were going to
make a manufacturing country out of it. But when the
commission which had been sent from Washington
returned, and brought back the glorious news, I was lifted
up in hope. A little dissatisfaction arose in annexing it, and
I saw it would be a failure. The minds of the people were
not ready to receive it, and they let that pass by, and they
have said no more about it that I have heard. There is
another thing that has often passed through my mind with
regard to Africa. I have a great idea about Africa.
Sometimes I think that it is the land the Bible speaks of as

flowing with milk and honey, although I have talked with a great many learned people, and they tell me that is not the country, but I have become confirmed in the belief that it is the glorious country. I have often thought the Lord did not intend that enlightened people should know much about the country. As far as I can learn, no history can tell how large the country is, or how many inhabitants there are. It seems to me as if the Lord had left a small tract of land open, to see how much wickedness man would do, and to see how much evil they would do to the inhabitants of that glorious country. It seemed as if the Lord had made Africa one of the richest and most glorious countries in the land. It seems as if there was so much evil in the land that it was destroyed, and the Lord has never allowed it to be built up again, that it has been left till some future time, when it will be used for the Lord's benefit. It seems as if God placed the colored people in that land to keep possession of it, and keep other countries from learning what is in the country, and from finding out the great riches that are in Africa. It is my opinion that it is the richest country that has ever been discovered, that it is too rich for enlightened people to have possession of. It seems as if the colored people are not as ingenious as the white people are in prying into earthly things. I think God has laid down many laws to the inhabitants, which they thoroughly understand, but we do not. I often thought that if a famine was to come on the world, it would never hurt Africa. I have often thought that if a great war was to come over the land, it would not affect Africa, though they have torn down one great evil in the land, but there is a greater evil still growing up in the land, and it is spreading all over the land, and this evil it seems impossible to touch or get at it at the present time, though thousands feel it. Sometimes I think that evil will be the cause of nations being destroyed. It makes a great play in the land, and is the cause of a great many people following on after it. The same evil is running along on the borders of Africa, and the same evil is spreading in a great many other countries, but I do not think the Lord intended it to get very far back in Africa. I often think that before the end of time, the colored people will return again to their own country, and I think there will be a great light shown to them in the future, that they might thoroughly understand. I never heard of their emigrating from their own country to any other, and I think they never will. As for my part, I have hard feelings against no person, although my race have been cheated out of all their labor, and many are lying in the ground waiting till the last day when the Lord will call on them to arise, then they will lay all their troubles before Him. But God knows all about it, He has the law fixed. Many have lived to receive their liberty from man, who turned them loose without giving them anything. A great many people make remarks about colored people being ignorant and not taking care of themselves, but if they look at it right, will see that we never had a chance to, because we have been shut out from all the privileges of the land.

The colored people did not have wealthy parents to send them to school to learn the sciences of the earth, and that is the reason they are uneducated to-day. There is a ray of light streaming through the land at the present day, showing the colored people they have some true friends, whose minds the Lord has blessed, that they might show kind feelings to an oppressed race of people, and that has borne them up to this day. There are a great many that know the true Spirit of God, and the manner and way they must live. The Lord has shown me a light in other days. I always believed there was great wisdom to be received from on high, though I have an evil, heart to contend with I shall be faithful in overcoming that evil, that I may obtain the great prize. The Lord has shown me many things, and has given me understanding. I passed through many things when in bondage. I had great troubles and trials, but the Lord ministered to my heart and bore me up for the future. I studied what plan and steps could be taken to destroy slavery. I laid the plans that I thought could be taken to destroy it, but I will not mention them in this book. But before I had accomplished my plans, God put an end to it. I thought I was working through the Lord's wisdom, but I will let those days pass, they have gone never to return and look to the future. I see great work before me to accomplish. I must understand the sciences of the earth, and I am writing this book on purpose that I may get an education. The better a man understands the wisdom of the earth, he will be more humble to God, he will understand heavenly things. If it is the Lord's will, I believe I shall accomplish it, and if is not His will, I shall not. Many will ask the reason why I have not been to school, but I will leave that question and answer it at some future day, if it is the Lord's will. I trust I have laid up riches in heaven, if I am only humble in the Lord's grace, though a man ought to do all the good, he can in this world, and after he has done that, it is but a small thing in the sight of God. Then shall the dust return to the earth, and the Spirit shall return unto God who gave it. For God shall bring everything to judgment, with every secret thing, whether it be good or whether it be evil.

www.ingramcontent.com/pod-product-compliance
Lightning Source LLC
Chambersburg PA
CBHW030853090426
42737CB00009B/1213